BUSHCRAFT ILLUSTRATED

— A VISUAL GUIDE —

Dave Canterbury

New York Times Bestselling Author of *Bushcraft 101*

ADAMS MEDIA

New York   London   Toronto   Sydney   New Delhi

For my brother-in-law
James Martin Samuel Dykes
"Hippaugh"
April 11, 1973–October 29, 2017

And to anyone and everyone suffering from or affected by depression,
mental illness, substance abuse, or suicide.

Adams Media
An Imprint of Simon & Schuster, LLC
100 Technology Center Drive
Stoughton, MA 02072

First Adams Media hardcover edition May 2019

ADAMS MEDIA and colophon are trademarks of Simon &
Schuster.

For information about special discounts for bulk purchases,
please contact Simon & Schuster Special Sales at 1-866-506-
1949 or business@simonandschuster.com.

The Simon & Schuster Speakers Bureau can bring authors
to your live event. For more information or to book an
event contact the Simon & Schuster Speakers Bureau at
1-866-248-3049 or visit our website at
www.simonspeakers.com.

Interior design by Frank Rivera and Colleen Cunningham
Interior illustrations by Eric Andrews; Claudia Wolf;
MDC Staff, courtesy Missouri Department of Conservation

Manufactured in China

1 0 9 8 7 6 5

Library of Congress Cataloging-in-Publication Data
Names: Canterbury, Dave, author.
Title: Bushcraft illustrated / Dave Canterbury, New
York Times bestselling author of Bushcraft 101.
Description: Avon, Massachusetts: Adams Media, 2019.
Series: Bushcraft.
Includes index.
Identifiers: LCCN 2018033603 (print) | LCCN
2018033996 (ebook) | ISBN 9781507209028 (hc) |
ISBN 9781507209066 (ebook)
Subjects: LCSH: Wilderness survival--Handbooks,
manuals, etc. | Outdoor life--Handbooks, manuals, etc. |
Outdoor recreation--Handbooks, manuals, etc. | Camping-
-Handbooks, manuals, etc. | Camping--Equipment
and supplies--Handbooks, manuals, etc.
Classification: LCC GV200.5 (ebook) | LCC GV200.5
.C374 2018 (print) | DDC 613.6/9--dc23
LC record available at https://lccn.loc.gov/2018033603

ISBN 978-1-5072-0902-8
ISBN 978-1-5072-0906-6 (ebook)

Many of the designations used by manufacturers and sellers to
distinguish their products are claimed as trademarks. Where
those designations appear in this book and Simon & Schuster,
Inc., was aware of a trademark claim, the designations have
been printed with initial capital letters.

Readers are urged to take all appropriate precautions before
undertaking any how-to task. Always read and follow
instructions and safety warnings for all tools and materials,
and call in a professional if the task stretches your abilities too
far. Although every effort has been made to provide the best
possible information in this book, neither the publisher nor
the author is responsible for accidents, injuries, or damage
incurred as a result of tasks undertaken by readers. This book
is not a substitute for professional services.

Contains material adapted from the following titles published
by Adams Media, an Imprint of Simon & Schuster, Inc.:
Bushcraft 101 by Dave Canterbury, copyright © 2014, ISBN
978-1-4405-7977-6; The Bushcraft Field Guide to Trapping,
Gathering, & Cooking in the Wild by Dave Canterbury,
copyright © 2016, ISBN 978-1-4405-9852-4; Bushcraft First
Aid by Dave Canterbury and Jason A. Hunt, PhD, copyright
© 2017, ISBN 978-1-5072-0234-0.

Contents

Introduction   7

— Introduction —

BUSHCRAFT COMES FROM a desire to reconnect with nature. It's the skills you need to be able to use what you have in the outdoors to help you survive. This book is an illustrated guide to help you acquire that knowledge, showing you exactly how these tools and skills can be used.

It is important in bushcraft to be fully aware of the natural world around you. I often tell my students to become a naturalist first and a bushcrafter second. That's because so much of what you need to survive in the wilderness is provided by the wilderness itself. Naturalists and authors like Richard Graves and Mors Kochanski who helped develop the practice meant for bushcraft to be a set of skills that allowed you to effectively create what you need from what you're able to find.

Carrying a simple survival kit is always the best plan. You'll be able to bring these items with you in order to work with the materials you find. This book catalogs the most beneficial items you'll want to carry into the woods as they're more difficult to reproduce from natural materials.

You will then use what you packed to create what you need. You will focus on crafting a myriad of necessities—from traps to shelter to other useful campsite items. Making traps and other food-gathering devices helps to supplement and cut down on the food you need to pack. Building shelter out of natural materials helps you reconnect with nature since you won't have to sleep in tents made of synthetic fabrics. Crafting campsite items makes things more convenient, cutting down on the gear you need to carry and allowing you to replace any damaged gear.

While I have no aversion to the latest and best in modern technology, I find that many times it takes away from the experience of being in the wild. Through the illustrations and instructions included in this book, you should learn about the basic gear and skills you will need to enjoy the wilderness as it is intended. To truly connect with nature requires us to be close to it. While these skills can be used in a bushcraft trip into the woods, you can also use and perfect them in your own backyard or park while camping, canoeing, hunting, fishing, or even homesteading.

I hope you will enjoy this book and your time in nature and, remember, it is always best to be prepared.

—*Dave Canterbury*

CHAPTER 1

PACKS

THERE ARE, OF COURSE, certain elements of kit that we carry into the woods, even though, in the spirit of bushcraft, we prefer to make them from the landscape. I generally prefer to carry only a few items in and make what I need otherwise. After all, this is the essence of bushcraft. But not everyone has the land, resources, or ability to make every single shelter and bed from scratch, nor do we always have the time to make clay pots to cook food in prior to needing to eat. So some items should always be carried in the pack to keep you going.

You should never be fooled into thinking that carrying in kit means you are not practicing bushcraft. You can still make cook utensils, harvest wild edibles, catch and kill wild meat sources, create camp stools and chairs, create a candle holder or lamp hook from a tree fork, or build a tripod to hang your pot. All these things are also bushcraft.

A pack is truly one of the things that is best carried in, but that does not necessarily mean it cannot be made from natural materials later. It could even be put together as a DIY project. I look at the pack as another container, except for carrying tools instead of water or food. In this chapter, I'll show you some of my favorite types of packs, and I'll give you some instructions on how to make your own.

CHOOSE A PACK

When you're choosing a pack, you'll want something that can contain your kit but isn't too complicated to use. I am a big fan of simplicity and the pack you use does not have to be the fanciest design or the latest and greatest lightweight fabric and technological suspension system. Any canvas bag will work fine. You can also fashion a pack frame easily and attach a simple canvas sack to it in the beginning if you choose to.

I like bucket-style packs myself as it makes things easy to find and you don't get confused on where you put something in the ten pockets and zippered pouches many new packs seem to have. A couple of outside pockets can work well for things you may need on the fly like fire kits, folding saws, or cordages. I like two or three outside side pockets large enough for tools in one side and a water bottle in the other. A pouch in the front gives ready access to a fire kit and gloves. Everything else goes in the main pack.

Old Forest Service packs or Boy Scout packs are easy enough to come by fairly cheap and if they are in disrepair can be fixed by your own hand, or they make a great pattern to work off of for making your own pack. See **FIGURES 1.1a–1.1f** to get an idea of the different types of packs.

DULUTH PACK

Figure 1.1a

▲ The Duluth pack is a traditional pack used by woodsmen since the 1800s. It is usually made of heavy canvas with an open bucket. It offers durability and simplicity but is a bit heavy.

DUFFEL BAG

Figure 1.1b

▲ The military-style duffel bag offers an inexpensive and easy-to-find bucket-style pack with a large amount of space. This pack, however, would not be the best choice for the camper on foot because it is more awkward to carry than other choices.

PACK BOARD

Figure 1.1c

▲ Pack boards offer a good weight distribution over the surface of your back and allow for attachment of many different articles and packs as well as ease of carrying out game on a hunt.

NORWEGIAN MEIS

Figure 1.1d

▲ Meis is Norwegian for "bag with a frame" and is what it sounds like, a bag tied to a wooden frame.

RUCKSACK

Figure 1.1e

▲ The rucksack, typically now called a backpack, carries items on the back in an organized fashion. Outside pockets help make gear such as fire kits, gloves, and headlights immediately accessible.

YUCCA PACK

Figure 1.1f

▲ Yucca packs are good starter packs and have been used by the Boy Scouts of America. It's a simple but effective design.

— MAKING PACKS —

It is also entirely possible to fold your kit into your tarp and make a pack. See **FIGURE** 1.2.

Pack straps are a simple way to use a tarp or other large sheet to roll your complete camp setup into. Attach a set of straps to form a backpack. See **FIGURE** 1.3.

MAKING A PACK FROM A TARP

PACK STRAPS

1.   2.

3.

Figure 1.2

Figure 1.3

MAKING A CANVAS PACK You may also want to make your own backpack, using sturdy canvas, as shown in **FIGURE 1.4**. Making a backpack from natural materials can be a time-consuming process and very material dependent. However, you have all the time in the world to make one if you choose.

MAKING A CANVAS PACK

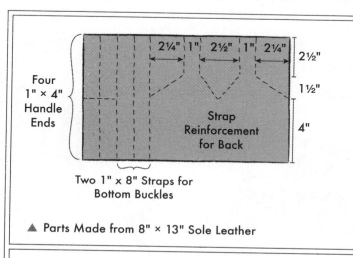

▲ Parts Made from 8" × 13" Sole Leather

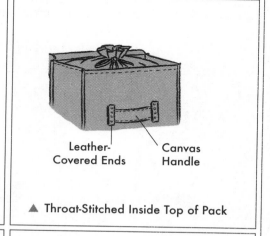

▲ Throat-Stitched Inside Top of Pack

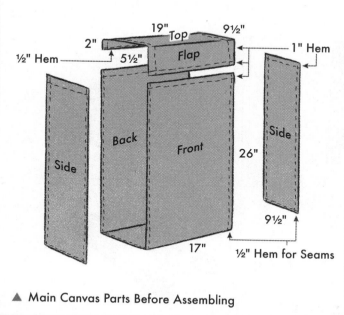

▲ Main Canvas Parts Before Assembling

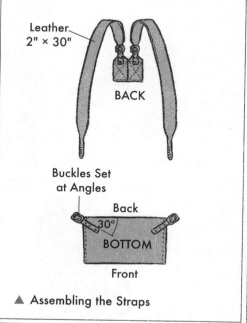

▲ Assembling the Straps

Figure 1.4

External frames have been used since ancient times. They are great for supporting the load, and they work well for carrying other things like firewood or quartered game when not in use for the pack itself. Making wood frames is a great way to add a bushcraft touch to a modern pack. There are several types of frames you can make fairly easily. The following illustrations (**FIGURES 1.5 THROUGH 1.11**) show a few of them.

LADDER-BACK ALASKAN FRAME

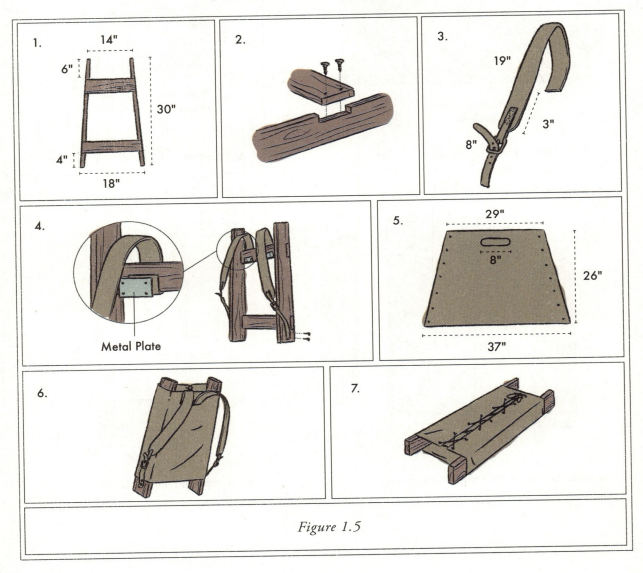

Figure 1.5

LADDER-BACK FRAME

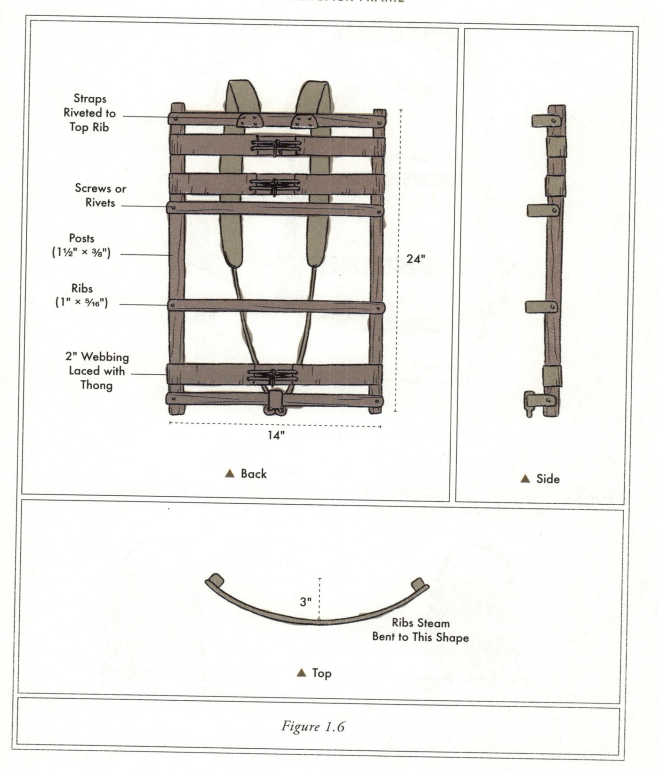

Straps Riveted to Top Rib

Screws or Rivets

Posts (1½" × ⅜")

Ribs (1" × ⁵⁄₁₆")

2" Webbing Laced with Thong

24"

14"

▲ Back

▲ Side

3"

Ribs Steam Bent to This Shape

▲ Top

Figure 1.6

SENECA FRAME

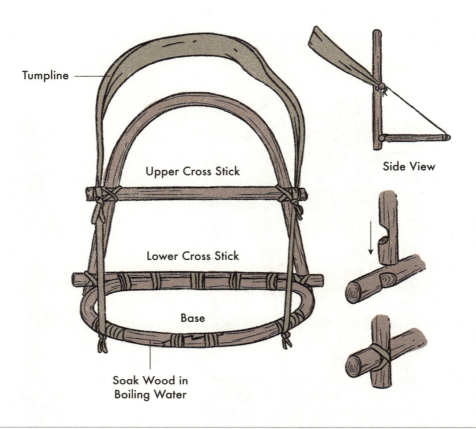

Tumpline

Upper Cross Stick

Side View

Lower Cross Stick

Base

Soak Wood in
Boiling Water

Figure 1.7

FRONT OF A WORLD WAR II–STYLE PACK ON A SENECA FRAME

Figure 1.8

BACK OF A WORLD WAR II–STYLE PACK ON A SENECA FRAME

Figure 1.9

ROYCRAFT FRAME

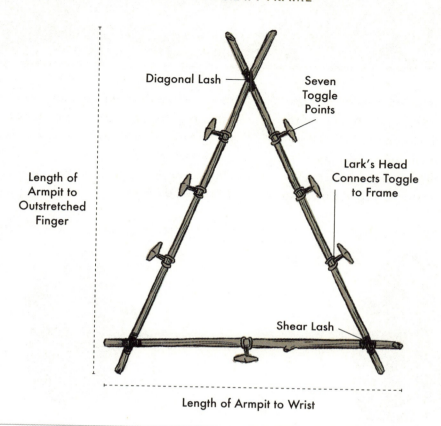

Diagonal Lash

Seven Toggle Points

Lark's Head Connects Toggle to Frame

Length of Armpit to Outstretched Finger

Shear Lash

Length of Armpit to Wrist

Figure 1.10

Y FRAME

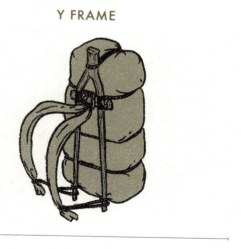

Figure 1.11

Bushcraft Tip

The most popular improvised frame today is the Roycraft frame, named after Tom Roycraft, an outdoorsman who taught the construction of this type of frame to Mors Kochanski, the famous Canadian bushcraft and wilderness survival expert. This simple triangle can be constructed within minutes and can last many years if the lashings are correct and the wood selection is wise.

Pack baskets are baskets with runners. Runners are slats of wood that protect the bottom of the pack when in contact with the ground. They are generally woven from ash splits and come in many sizes. They are typically fitted with either cotton webbing or leather for straps. The advantage to these packs is the rigid structure, which makes protecting contents a bit easier. However, you give up the advantage of the external frame and the soft pack that offers a sleeker profile and can be cinched smaller if less is packed in. See **FIGURES 1.12 THROUGH 1.14** for examples of pack baskets.

PACK BASKETS

Figure 1.12

ASH PACK BASKET WITH STRAP

Figure 1.13

PACK BASKET WITH FLAP

Figure 1.14

Bushcraft Tip

Pack baskets have been used for many years, starting with the fur trappers of the Hudson's Bay Company in the late 1600s. It's easy to put things in and retrieve them later, and since the baskets are generally made from wood or modern synthetics, they also drain well if anything you put in them is wet.

PACK BASKET MAKING

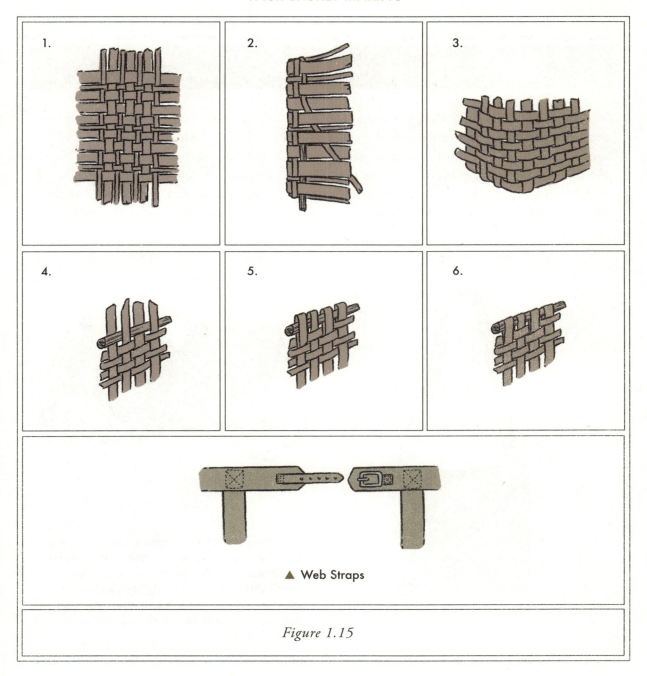

▲ Web Straps

Figure 1.15

⸺ IN ADDITION TO YOUR PACK ⸺

You may find some other items useful in carrying your kit, especially if you will be foraging or collecting natural resources.

HAVERSACK

A haversack is a small cloth or leather bag carried on one side of the body, usually with just one strap. The haversack has been a standard carry item since the days of the frontier. This device is used to carry items that are of immediate importance or items you collect along the journey. Never overstuff this bag to the point that you run out of room, especially for things you find along the trail; you may need room to store quick tinder sources or bird's nest material. See **FIGURE 1.16** for an example of a haversack and **FIGURE 1.17** for an example of what to carry in your haversack.

ONE-STRAP HAVERSACK

Figure 1.16

HAVERSACK KIT WITH PERSONAL CARRY ITEMS

Figure 1.17

▲ This haversack kit is carried along with a belt pouch (see following section for more information on belt pouches). This kit contains a stainless water bottle, kuksa, fire steel, hook knife, twisted metal fork, tarred hemp line, a piece of cotton material, carving knife, wooden spoon, and a leather tinder bag.

BELT POUCHES

Belt pouches, usually made of leather, are where the bushcrafter keeps the main fire kit and possibly a spare carving knife or jackknife. It is your wallet, so to speak, used to carry the most important items you may need, especially if you have left everything else behind at camp or if you lose your supplies. The size of this pouch can vary, but you don't want it so big as to become cumbersome while moving about; keep it simple by choosing a smaller version. **FIGURE 1.18** shows an example of a belt pouch with a variety of personal carry items.

ANOTHER BELT POUCH WITH DIFFERENT PERSONAL CARRY ITEMS

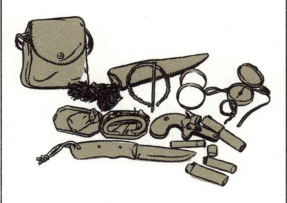

Figure 1.18

▲ This belt pouch contains a blanket pin, flint-and-steel kit, lighter, matches, compass, some tinder materials, and a magnification lens. The small derringer is pocket carried and the belt knife is worn beside the pouch.

TUMPLINES

Tumplines are straps attached to a heavier load (such as a pack or frame) that are worn across the forehead to assist in carrying the load. In this day and age with the new designs of modern packs, tumplines are, for the most part, unnecessary, but they can be useful if you're doing things in a more minimal fashion and are trying to get the most from your gear. I can tell you that a tumpline comes in very handy when trapping, since you may be carrying a basket filled with about 100 pounds of the day's catch, in addition to your equipment. This alone makes it worthwhile if you're planning to trap. See **FIGURE 1.19** for an example of a tumpline.

AN EXAMPLE OF A TUMPLINE FOR HELPING TO CARRY A LOAD

Figure 1.19

TOOLS

BUSHCRAFT CAN BE defined as our ability to fashion objects of need at any given time. We take advantage of nature's storehouses for necessities as they may not occur within our everyday kit or to repair/replace something damaged during our time in the woods. The essence of the word craft means to create. We can do rudimentary crafting with only the minimum of tools. Three of the most important tools are the knife, saw, and axe. While these three tools will do many things, having some others on hand will help immensely if you set out to process wood material into usable objects. You want to make sure you have the correct tool for the task at hand depending on the size of the project and your ability to transport the tools. In this chapter we will discuss a few of these tools and give examples of some of their uses.

⟶ PROCESSING WOOD ⟶

When you look at crafting from the landscape you will use wood to create more usable objects around camp than anything else. To process wood, you must do five things and you must carry tools that allow you to accomplish these five goals, with those tools dictated by the size of your kit, projects planned, and space and weight allowances. I call this the "Five-Tool Rule." Following is a list of the five wood-processing tasks and the tools most often used to accomplish them, and we will discuss further as we go.

1. Severing the grain: saw, axe, knife, mocotaugan, draw knife, spoon knife, gouge
2. Splitting the wood with the grain: axe, knife
3. Shaping the wood: axe, knife, mocotaugan
4. Boring the wood: knife, awl, auger
5. Making concavities: knife, mocotaugan, gouge, spoon knife

If you can accomplish these five things, you can successfully make almost anything you need, from a spoon to a cabin. Many of the tools we will discuss can perform multiple tasks but may only truly excel at a single task, working passably for others. Some may be designed to do multiple tasks.

In their smallest and easiest to carry form, the five tools most useful for processing wood include:

- Small belt knife
- Folding saw
- Hatchet
- Awl
- Spoon knife or mocotaugan (both used mainly for woodworking)

Looking at this list you will see one tool that should be able to accomplish all five tasks in passable fashion, and that is the knife. It is for this reason I teach that the belt knife is your most important tool and must be matched to these requirements. When processing wood, it must be able to sever and split firewood-sized material as well as shape and notch things as fine as a bow drill fire set.

— KNIVES —

An outdoor knife is the main tool used by most crafters to fashion items from the landscape. It is usually the first tool you will reach for when working around camp on smaller projects as well as being used to process your food. Most of us will carry more than one knife and most will carry other tools for larger tasks. First, it's important to discuss what a belt knife is and what makes a good belt knife as this tool seems to cause the most confusion to beginners.

Bushcraft Tip

If you are not alone in your excursion into the wild, any time you prepare to use your belt knife you will need to evaluate your blood circle. This is the area 360 degrees around you and farther than arm's length, where someone could come into contact with a blade being pushed away from the material being cut.

BELT KNIVES

Your belt knife is your main tool for bushcrafting and as such it really must be multifunctional in nature in and of itself. A knife that is too small will not be good for processing firewood if needed, and a knife that is too big will not be good for fine carving and shaping wood. One would hope to have all the tools listed on the previous page at any given time and, in this case, one can really refine the belt knife to a certain set of criteria, one that is more suited to the finer tasks; an axe and saw will do the heavy work. This may not always be the case and may not always be feasible, so it is best to stay in the 4"–5" range with a full tang and a carbon steel blade. This will give your knife maximum versatility.

See **FIGURE 2.1** for an illustration of the anatomy of a knife.

ANATOMY OF A KNIFE

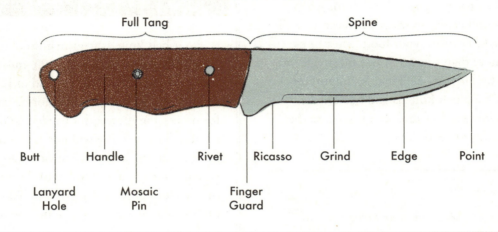

Figure 2.1

KNIFE TANGS

Many knives do not have a full tang, the part of the blade that extends into the handle of the knife, and while fully functional for most general uses, as well as being lighter in weight, in my eyes they are not the best blade for a belt knife or main tool due to the reduction in material width that may cause overall weakness, especially when used for things that require batoning like splitting and felling. See **FIGURE 2.2** for a chart of various knife tangs.

DIFFERENT KINDS OF KNIFE TANGS

◄ Full

◄ Skeletonized

◄ Partial

◄ Narrowing

◄ Stick

Figure 2.2

KNIFE BLADE TYPE/KNIFE PROFILE

Knife blade type (the knife profile) is really a matter of personal preference and the intended use of the blade. These different uses can be the reason for carrying more than one blade. See **FIGURE 2.3** for a chart showing various knife blades. The types of blades and the tasks they are best for include:

- Drop Point Blade, Trailing Point Blade, Modified Trailing Point Blade: skinning and game processing
- Straight Back Blade: most craft work
- Spear Point Blade: all-around use, for the camper
- Straight Edge Blade: best used for things like razors with a hollow grind
- Clip Point Blade: when piercing is needed

KNIFE GRIND/KNIFE EDGE

Knife grind is another feature that boils down to your intended use. While the full convex grind will be a durable knife and hold up well to things like batoning, it also has disadvantages over a Scandi grind when it comes to ease of honing or sharpening in the field as well as performing finer carving tasks. Other grinds will generally have a main grind and a secondary bevel with the flat grind and can be a good compromise. Hollow grinds are generally reserved for smaller blades like multi-tool and pocket knives, and while they can be extremely sharp they will not withstand the side-to-side stress of other grinds. See **FIGURE 2.4** for various knife edges.

VARIOUS KNIFE BLADES

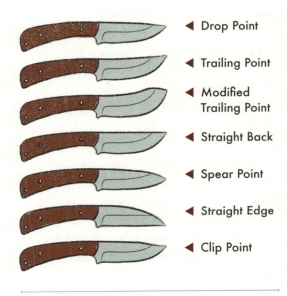

◀ Drop Point

◀ Trailing Point

◀ Modified Trailing Point

◀ Straight Back

◀ Spear Point

◀ Straight Edge

◀ Clip Point

Figure 2.3

VARIOUS KNIFE EDGES

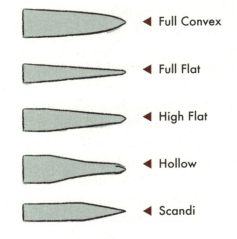

◀ Full Convex

◀ Full Flat

◀ High Flat

◀ Hollow

◀ Scandi

Figure 2.4

You should be able to accomplish five main tasks with your belt knife:

1. Creating fire lay materials
2. Starting a fire
3. Cutting saplings
4. Felling a tree
5. Creating notches

That said, many knife-craft skills are important, and many overlap each other in some way. Therefore, the items on this list of skills are the ones I believe to have the most direct effect in an emergency if you are left with only having your trusty belt knife as a tool. To that end fire and shelter will be more important to you than most other things, so the skills you must initially own are based on this premise.

1. CREATING FIRE LAY MATERIALS

You'll use your knife to create fire lay materials (firecraft itself is discussed further in Chapter 6). There are three elements of any fire lay: tinder, kindling, and fuel. With this in mind you have to look at how your knife can be used to process all three effectively and safely, while still bearing in mind the tool itself is a resource to be conserved as much as possible. The number one rule in our conservation theory is don't use your knife unless you have to. Look for wood of the correct size to create kindling and fuel that is just lying about the forest floor.

Now of course many times the best things will either not be available or be in an unusable condition when we need them most, so you will need to use your knife. For creating tinder materials you want to find inner barks of trees like cedar or poplar if possible. These will be highly combustible and can be worked by hand once harvested to create the bird's nest or tinder bundle, as described in Chapter 6.

You want to avoid as much as possible using the blade of your knife for this process and so a 90-degree sharp spine—which means the spine is squared off to be sharp on the corners, not unlike a cabinet scraper—becomes a sure bonus for your sheath knife. You can also use this 90-degree spine to shave smaller stick materials like fatwood and softer species to create fine shavings that can be used as kindling and have less effect on the knife by conserving the blade edge as well. See **FIGURE 2.5** for an example of using a knife to shave tinder.

SHAVING TINDER MATERIALS

Figure 2.5

For kindling material and fuel wood we may need to baton, or strike the back of the tool or knife with a wooden mallet or baton for processing, the blade of our knife to split material along the grain to reduce the diameter as well as possibly baton across the grain to reduce the length if we cannot simply break it by hand or use the fork of a tree for leverage to snap the length. See **FIGURE 2.6** for an example of batoning with a knife.

BATONING WITH A KNIFE

Figure 2.6

Batoning is an indispensable skill if you are ever left with only a knife to process wood. First, try to use material that is free of knots and small in diameter, and if possible, do not use a knife without a full tang. When you need to baton to split the grain, keep impact blows in the center of the blade and centered in the material. Once you have initially split the grain, you should be able to place a wooden wedge of material in the split and baton that to complete the task.

A good rule of thumb for splitting is to never split a log that is so large it will not allow at least an inch of the side of the blade to protrude from the split once the knife disappears into the split. If you have to strike the knife again, strike the tip, never the handle. Have some sort of anvil under the material in case the knife goes cleanly through a split. This prevents the blade from striking the ground, causing potential damage.

2. STARTING A FIRE

Your knife is an important part of your fire-starting capability when it comes to combustion. You can use its spine to strike a ferrocerium rod, which is a mixed metal rod containing pyrophoric elements like iron and magnesium that produce hot sparks when materials are quickly scraped from the rod with a sharp object harder than the rod. It is also possible to use your knife as a steel for flint-and-steel ignition (provided you are using a high-carbon steel blade). See **FIGURE 2.7** for examples of ferrocerium rods.

VARIOUS FERROCERIUM RODS

Figure 2.7

Using the back 90-degree spine of the knife to strike a ferrocerium rod accomplishes several important and often overlooked things. First, it means you do not have to worry about carrying a separate striker, most of which are inadequate for the task anyway. You can get much better leverage on your knife to strike the rod. The true function of the ferrocerium rod is to be used as an emergency ignition tool, so you want the maximum amount of material to be removed from the rod with a single strike (this is the reason I believe a soft, large rod is better than a smaller or harder rod of this type). You can bring maximum power and maximize the surface area being pushed against the rod with a knife blade. See **FIGURES 2.8 AND 2.9** for examples of striking a ferrocerium rod. For an example of a flint-and-steel kit, see **FIGURE 2.10**.

STRIKING A FERROCERIUM ROD, VERSION 1

Figure 2.8

STRIKING A FERROCERIUM ROD, VERSION 2

Figure 2.9

FLINT-AND-STEEL KIT

Figure 2.10

3. CUTTING SAPLINGS

Cutting saplings becomes necessary for shelter building as green wood may be preferable. The flexibility of green wood has distinct advantages when making dome-type structures. Cutting a sapling is as easy as taking advantage of the tree's own weaknesses. Bend the sapling over, stressing the fibers, and cut into them at an angle toward the root ball. See **FIGURE 2.11** for an example.

CUTTING A SAPLING

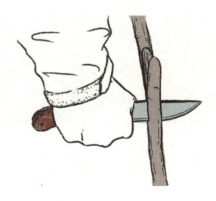

Figure 2.11

4. FELLING A TREE

When we talk about felling a tree with a knife we are obviously not felling a fifty-year-old tree that would require an axe or axe/saw combination. Rather we're talking about felling trees of more manageable sizes, typically up to 4–5" in diameter that, unlike saplings, are not able to just be bent over and shear cut. For this discussion of what boils down to emergency knife use, you only need to harvest material that is large enough in diameter to be structural or good fuel. This technique is also known as beaver chewing, where you will baton your blade, creating a V notch around the tree, steadily reducing the diameter until you can push the tree over for further use or processing. See **FIGURES 2.12 AND 2.13** for examples of felling a tree.

FELLING A TREE

Figure 2.12

FELLING A TREE IN STEPS

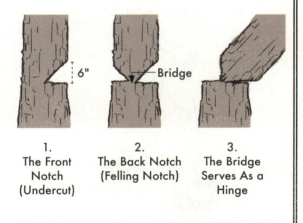

1.
The Front
Notch
(Undercut)

2.
The Back Notch
(Felling Notch)

3.
The Bridge
Serves As a
Hinge

Figure 2.13

5. CREATING NOTCHES

Notching of material is used for everything from building a structure to manipulating a pot over fire to creating trap components. Think about the Lincoln Logs you may have had as a youngster. The simple notches are what held everything together without the use of cordage or other fasteners. You may combine cord with a notch to better bind them but the notch makes interlocking of wood components possible. In my mind the most important yet rudimentary notches are the 7 notch, the log cabin notch, and the V notch. With these three simple notches many other things can be constructed. See **FIGURES 2.14 THROUGH 2.16** for examples.

THE 7 NOTCH

Figure 2.14

V NOTCH

Figure 2.15

V NOTCH

Figure 2.16

OTHER TYPES OF KNIVES

Once you realize the things your main knife may need to accomplish, you can look at other features of knives that you may find useful as well. This is where backup or secondary blades as well as things like Swiss Army knives and multi-tools come into play.

As with your belt knife, you will want to choose a folder with a blade profile most usable for your intended purpose. The advantage to many folders is the fact they may have multiple blade profiles in one tool, making them adaptable to several things at once. See **FIGURE 2.17** for a chart of blade types available in folding knives.

FOLDING KNIFE BLADES

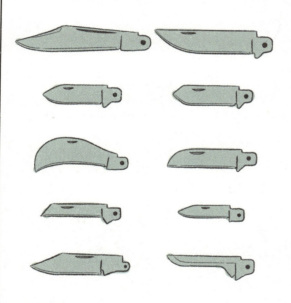

Figure 2.17

The hunter-style pocket knife by Case is good for field work with a larger blade for heavier skinning and cutting tasks and a bit slimmer and thinner blade for finer carving or gutting fish and fowl. See **FIGURE 2.18** for an example of this.

HUNTER'S POCKET KNIFE

Figure 2.18

The typical Scout-style knife carried by boys across the US for many decades adds a couple of useful camp tools like the can/bottle opener, screwdriver, as well as an awl for quick repair work. See **FIGURE 2.19** for an example of a Scout knife.

SCOUT KNIFE

Figure 2.19

Swiss Army knives have for years been the hiker's and camper's go-to for pocket carry. The inclusion of many useful tools, particularly the small folding saw, makes this a great addition to any kit. See **FIGURE 2.20** for an example of a Swiss Army knife.

SWISS ARMY KNIFE

Figure 2.20

HANDLING A FOLDING KNIFE

1.

▲ To open, hold in left hand and put right thumbnail into nail slot.

2.

▲ Pull blade out while pushing against hinge with little finger of left hand.

3.

▲ Continue to hold on to handle and blade until the blade snaps into open position.

4.

▲ To close, hold handle in left hand with fingers safely on the side.

5.

▲ Push against the back of the blade with the fingers of the right hand and swing handle up to meet the blade.

6.

▲ Let the knife snap shut. The "kick" at the base of the blade prevents edge from hitting the inside of handle.

Figure 2.21

MULTI-TOOLS

The main advantage to multi-tools, which are a fairly recent addition to the equipment list of many outdoorsmen, is the inclusion of a pair of pliers and wire cutters. Some of these tools also have a file handy for removing a nick from a hatchet and helping keen the edge. See **FIGURE 2.22** for an example of a multi-tool.

MULTI-TOOL

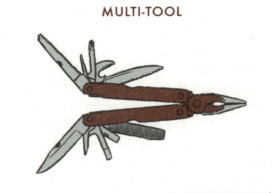

Figure 2.22

LARGE KNIVES

I find three types of larger knives to be excellent companion tools, especially in more southern parts of the US. Many times, especially in the late spring and summer months, these knives are superior to the axe.

A machete is a typical jungle tool, having a longer, more flexible blade than most knives. A good machete is easy to sharpen and should have a nice ring when tapped against solid wood. The advantage to the thinner cutting blade will become obvious for vines and river canes. It can also be used for some fairly fine craft work in experienced hands. See **FIGURE 2.23** for an example of a machete.

MACHETE

Figure 2.23

A parang is a thicker blade, generally at least ³⁄₁₆" with a slender design near the handle. It is used in many jungle environments because of its heft. It makes a great tool for not only light brush work but also for wood chopping tasks where a machete may not have enough weight in the blade for heavier work. Like the machete, a parang in the right hands can do amazing things. See **FIGURE 2.24** for an example of a parang.

Billhooks are tools used more commonly in the UK than in the US, but they deserve mention here as they can be a great tool. The hook-shaped blade makes this a very versatile tool not only for limbing tasks but also for chopping in general. The thickness of most billhook blades ranges between that of the machete and parang. Some billhooks have another chopping-type blade on the spine of the tool that can be used for small splitting tasks. See **FIGURE 2.25** for an example of a billhook.

PARANG

Figure 2.24

BILLHOOK

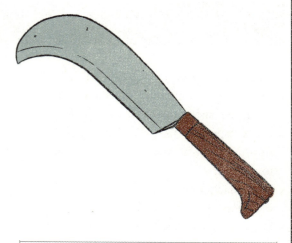

Figure 2.25

When using your knife there are a few safe knife grips to understand. The basic grips are the hammer grip, chest lever grip, and knee lever grip. See **FIGURES 2.26 THROUGH 2.28** for examples of these grips.

HAMMER GRIP

Figure 2.26

▲ A hammer grip is a power grip that keeps your fingers in a safe position when removing bulk amounts of material.

Bushcraft Tip

Safe handling practices with your knife in the field are of utmost importance. For this reason, place your belt knife immediately back into its sheath when you're not using it. Never place it on the ground or on another piece of gear.

CHEST LEVER GRIP

Figure 2.27

▲ Chest lever is a very controlled grip that will remove bulk materials as well as do finer work and, because the work is closer, you can see fine details better.

KNEE LEVER GRIP

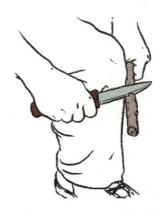

Figure 2.28

▲ Knee lever is another power or fine grip hold intended to maintain control of both the knife and the work for safety, but it allows you to hold the knife stationary while pulling the work piece to maintain an angle for fine work.

Steel is created with a combination of iron and carbon. If no other elements are added, the steel is called plain carbon steel. Steels used for knife blades have had other elements added in; these types of steels are called alloy steels. Alloy steels that have additional elements to make them resistant to corrosion in the wilderness are called stainless steels.

All non-stainless steel blades will need to be oiled to protect them from rust. I use food grade oil like mineral oil so that I can use the blade in food prep as well. However, oxidization or controlled rust is called patina and carbon blades will develop this over time, no matter how much they are oiled. In addition to oiling, when it comes to blade edge care, there are really several steps involved depending on how much wear the blade has taken prior to being maintained.

STROPPING

If you make your own paddle strop, which is better for a non-convex edge anyway, you can add compound, a clay-based paste used to add grit to a leather strop, to one side and use the other for final honing and buffing of the edge. See **FIGURE 2.29** for an example of a paddle strop.

PADDLE STROP

Figure 2.29

CERAMIC RODS

Using ceramic rods alone or in a V configuration in a wooden block is another nonaggressive way to fine-tune your edge. See **FIGURE 2.30**.

CERAMIC ROD SHARPENER

Figure 2.30

STEPS TO HONING YOUR BLADE Stropping, using leather to sharpen the edge of your knife, is the best technique for honing your blade back to a razor's edge. You will want to do this after every hard use as this will avoid the need to sharpen on a stone with a diamond sharpener (discussed in the following sections) or a ceramic rod. You can do this with a stropping paddle or with a loose leather strop like a belt. Adding a clay-based grit compound will assist in the process but will remove some metal (although much less than other methods). See **FIGURE 2.31** for the steps to honing your blade.

HONING YOUR BLADE

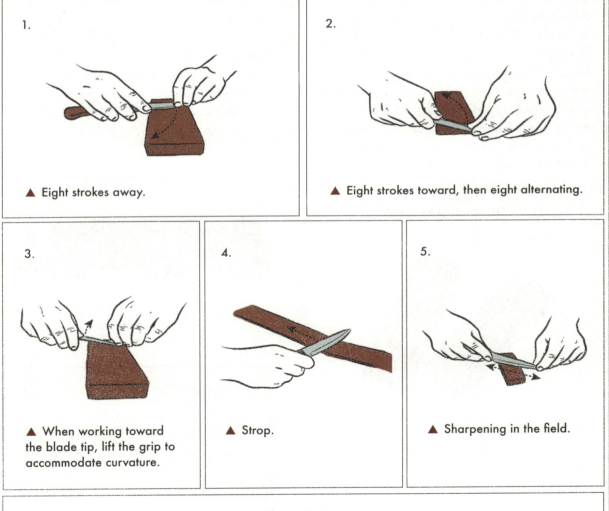

1.

▲ Eight strokes away.

2.

▲ Eight strokes toward, then eight alternating.

3.

▲ When working toward the blade tip, lift the grip to accommodate curvature.

4.

▲ Strop.

5.

▲ Sharpening in the field.

Figure 2.31

DIAMOND SHARPENERS

Diamond sharpeners come in many forms, from a flat card to a flat handle with a small diamond sharpener at the end, as well as in the shape of a small whetstone, depending on brand. Some have multiple grits on either side as well. These tools are good for a quick field sharpening if your knife has gone beyond the stropping stage. Remember that diamond is grit and at this point you will be removing metal from the blade, which, over repeated use, shortens the life of the blade overall. The convenience of these sharpeners and the multiple sizes available makes them a good choice for the pack. Some versions have diamond on one side and ceramic on the other. See **FIGURE 2.32** for an example.

TWO-SIDED SHARPENER

Figure 2.32

WATERSTONES AND WHETSTONES

Waterstones and whetstones are types of sharpening tools that sharpen your blades by grinding. Waterstones are generally made from a sedimentary rock and absorb water, which makes a great lubricant for the stones. You never want to use oil on a waterstone. Whetstones, whether a bench stone or pocket stone, can be lubricated with water or oil but are generally used with oil. I prefer to use water on all my stones as they are easier to clean when they get clogged with filings and water is easily accessible in the wild. See **FIGURE 2.33** for an example of a stone in a holder.

STONE IN HOLDER

Figure 2.33

Bushcraft Tip

Traditionally most whetstones were lubricated with oil, but water is a better option. Remember, if you use oil even once, you can never go back to using water.

SILICON CARBIDE

Silicon carbide sharpeners are best used with oil. They are coarser and more suited for machetes and axes than knives. They sometimes come in the shape of a propeller to be used on gardening tools. Many of the stones used to resurface or flatten a waterstone are made from silicon carbide and are used dry. See **FIGURE 2.34** for an example of this type of stone and **FIGURE 2.35** for an example of it in use.

PROPELLER STONE

Figure 2.34

PROPELLER STONE IN USE

Figure 2.35

KNIFE SHARPENING NOTES

When you're sharpening any knife (or axe), it is a good idea to color the entire area you wish to make contact with the stone (the bevel) with a black marker. This will help you see that you are hitting the right areas and all areas evenly on the stone. See **FIGURE 2.36** for sharpening angles.

KNIFE SHARPENING ANGLES

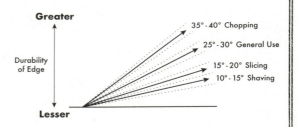

Figure 2.36

As you switch from one side to the other of the blade you will raise a burr on one side, then remove it on the other. You want this burr completely gone when finished for a true and keen edge. See **FIGURE 2.37** for an example of how the burr occurs.

KNIFE WITH BURR

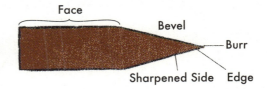

Figure 2.37

AXES, HATCHETS, AND HAWKS

These edged tools may be among the most trusted in your lineup. A favorite axe fits like a favorite pair of gloves. The size of this tool is truly dependent on your environment, the terrain, and materials to be processed.

ANATOMY OF AN AXE

See **FIGURE 2.38** for the anatomy of an axe.

ANATOMY OF AN AXE

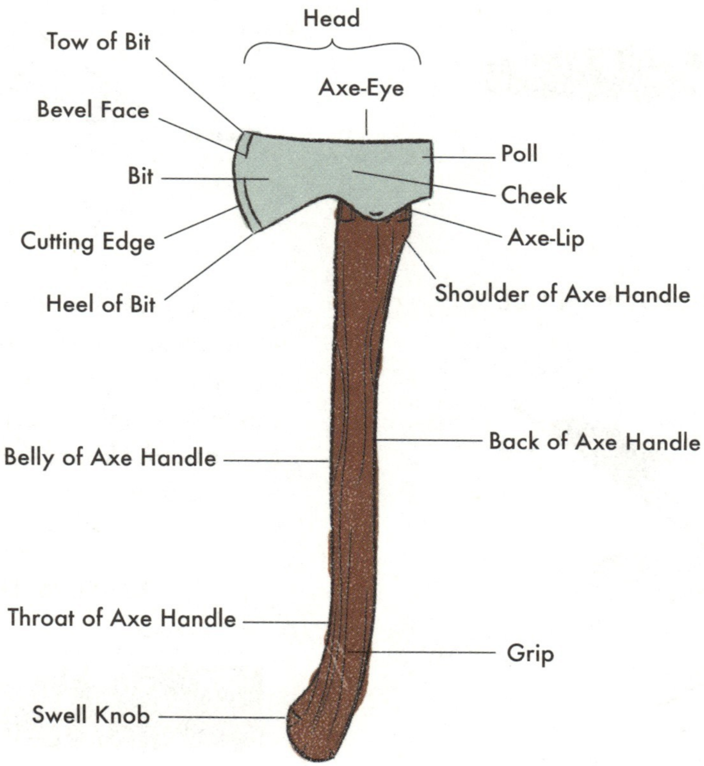

Head

Tow of Bit

Axe-Eye

Bevel Face

Bit

Poll

Cheek

Cutting Edge

Axe-Lip

Heel of Bit

Shoulder of Axe Handle

Back of Axe Handle

Belly of Axe Handle

Throat of Axe Handle

Grip

Swell Knob

Figure 2.38

AXE HANDLES

The axe handle comes in various types. A straight handle generally adds to better control, while a curved handle adds to power. See **FIGURE 2.39** for examples.

It's convenient to make measurement marks on the axe handle so that you will have a handy ruler with you at all times. See **FIGURE 2.40** for an example of measurements burned into an axe handle.

AXE HANDLES

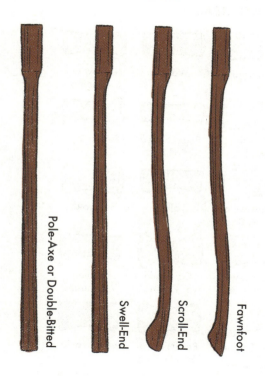

Pole-Axe or Double-Bitted

Swell-End

Scroll-End

Fawnfoot

Figure 2.39

MEASUREMENT MARKS

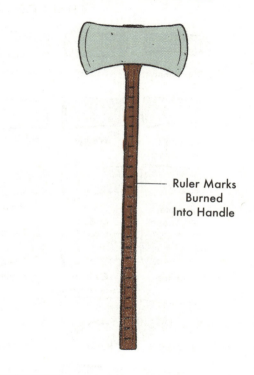

Ruler Marks
Burned
Into Handle

Figure 2.40

Axe heads were manufactured in various areas, and many were named for those areas of development. The type of head you choose is personal preference. However, the main types of longer axes are poled single bit and double bit. Double bit axes generally feature two different bevels so that one side can be used for grubbing or work near the ground and around knots, while the other is kept keen for limbing and felling tasks. The pole of the axe sometimes comes hardened and these are best for striking metal objects like wedges. See **FIGURE 2.41** for a chart showing types of axe heads.

CHART OF VARIOUS AXE HEADS

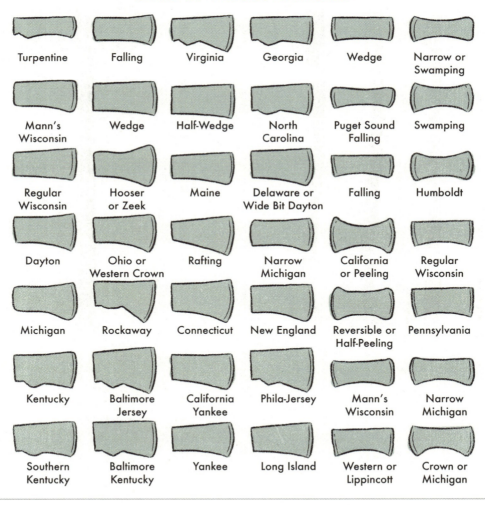

Figure 2.41

You can carry your axe and keep the blade covered using one of the sheath styles pictured in **FIGURE 2.42**.

AXE SHEATHS

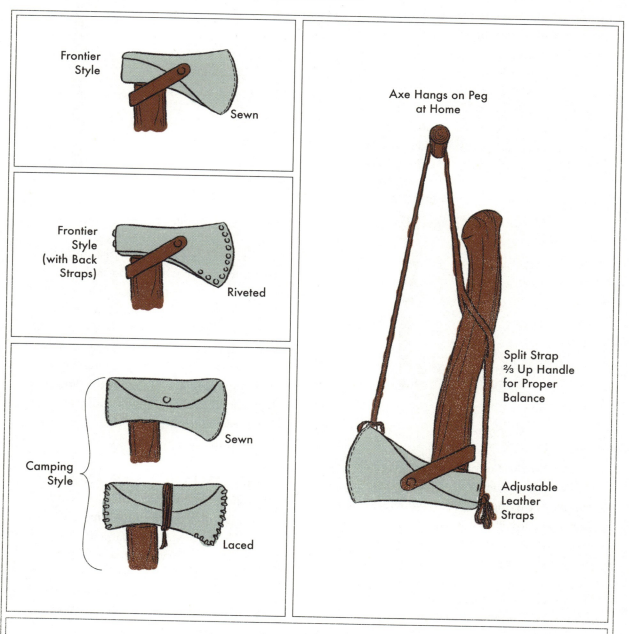

Frontier Style — Sewn

Frontier Style (with Back Straps) — Riveted

Camping Style — Sewn / Laced

Axe Hangs on Peg at Home

Split Strap ⅔ Up Handle for Proper Balance

Adjustable Leather Straps

Figure 2.42

For general needs, a two-pound boy's axe size is plenty large enough for general bushcraft. Unless you plan to build a cabin you most likely will need nothing bigger. I tend to carry the Council Tool woodcraft axe or the Gransfors Bruks forest axe more than the others. I have the small forest axe and it can be very handy as a pack axe being about the right size to ride neatly on most three-day packs or hiker's packs. **FIGURE 2.43** is the pack axe I like to carry.

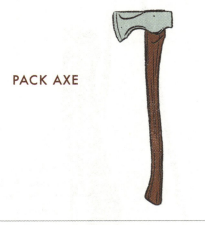

PACK AXE

Figure 2.43

Hatchets and tomahawks are generally similar in size unless they are a specialty tool like a carving axe, but the main advantage to the tomahawk is the handle replacement ease. It's a friction fit handle that goes in from the top of the eye with no wedge, whereas the hatchet handle will be fit into the bottom and wedged into place permanently. See **FIGURE 2.44** for an example of a tomahawk.

TOMAHAWK

Figure 2.44

That said, a good hatchet is a tough tool to beat. It has a bit more weight than most hawks and is just about right for crafting as well as making quick fire materials. However, if you are going to the woods specifically to craft and are weight conscious, many of the axe heads shown earlier in **FIGURE 2.41** can fit the same hawk handle, taking up less room and being very convenient if handles need to be fabricated.

SPECIALTY TYPES OF AXES

When selecting an axe for a certain task it is worth considering some specialty axes like the hewing axe, carpenter's axe, or carving axe. A carving axe will generally have more curvature to the blade and is used for woodcraft projects for removing the bulk of the waste. See **FIGURE 2.45** for an example of a carving axe.

CARVING AXE

Figure 2.45

A carpenter's axe is the opposite, with a straight edge blade. These axes generally have a straight edge instead of the typical curve, and they are used for things like hewing and shingle work with shakes. See **FIGURE 2.46**.

CARPENTER'S AXE

Figure 2.46

A hewing axe is beveled only on one side for making a smooth flat surface but not biting into the wood as it travels down the grain. See **FIGURE 2.47**.

HEWING AXE

Figure 2.47

Bushcraft Tip

The triangle of death is the space between your upper legs, including the groin and both femoral arteries. Avoid this area with an exposed knife, axe, or saw at all costs. Never cut into this area or hold objects to be cut or carved in a manner that could cause the blade to enter it.

There are many different ways to use an axe for accomplishing tasks so in this section we will only discuss what I consider safe practices for different bushcraft tasks.

When you decide to cut down a large tree with many branches you must choose the correct tree for the project at hand. Very seldom, unless you are cabin building, will you need to cut down a tree that's more than 6" in diameter. Ninety percent of the time 4" will suffice. After felling, the tree needs further processing to become usable. Limbing the tree involves removal of the limbs, some of which may be usable for other camp implements and improvised trapping, while the main tree may need to be bucked or cut into smaller, more manageable sizes for both transport and workability. See **FIGURES 2.48 THROUGH 2.54** for examples of some typical tasks an axe is used for, and illustrations of proper technique.

Bushcraft Tip

To figure out how tall a tree is, burn marks into the back of the axe handle in 1" increments. Take a measurement from the base of the tree, and tie a cord 5' up. Step away from the tree until you can capture that 5' of height within the 1" mark on your axe. See how many marks on the axe the tree is, and multiply that by 5' to get an approximate height.

AXE SWINGING HAND POSITIONS

Upward Swing

Downward Swing

Figure 2.48

FELLING A TREE

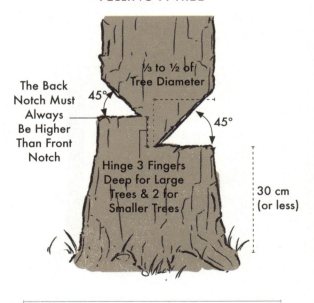

Figure 2.49

CHOPPING WITH AN AXE

Figure 2.50

PROPER CHOPPING ANGLES

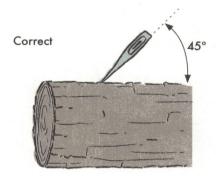

Correct

45°

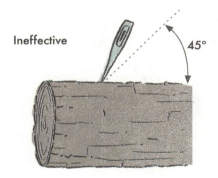

Ineffective

45°

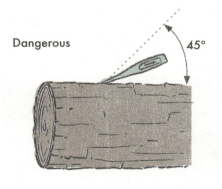

Dangerous

45°

Figure 2.51

LIMBING POSITION

Never branch on the near side.

Never straddle the log.

Figure 2.52

CORRECT ANGLE FOR LIMBING

Correct Direction

Incorrect Direction

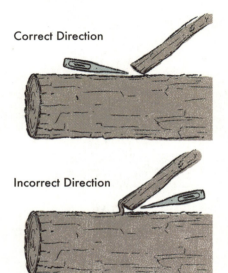

Figure 2.53

STRIKING SEQUENCE FOR BUCKING LARGE LOGS

Figure 2.54

Safely creating firewood materials will be one of the things you do the most often, and this is where many folks get hurt using the axe or end up damaging the handle or the blade itself. Never try to split wood for fires with an axe unless you have an anvil made of wood to stop the travel of the axe.

Always be aware of anything that may interfere with the travel of the axe on the downswing that could cause damage to the handle. The best position for splitting wood may be on your knees depending on the handle length of the chosen axe. **FIGURES 2.55 AND 2.56** show how to safely split wood. **FIGURE 2.57** shows how to safely hew wood.

SPLITTING A LOG

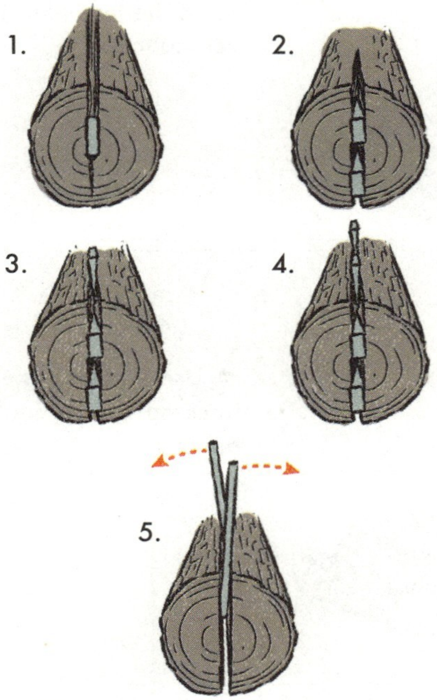

1.
2.
3.
4.
5.

Figure 2.55

SPLITTING FIREWOOD

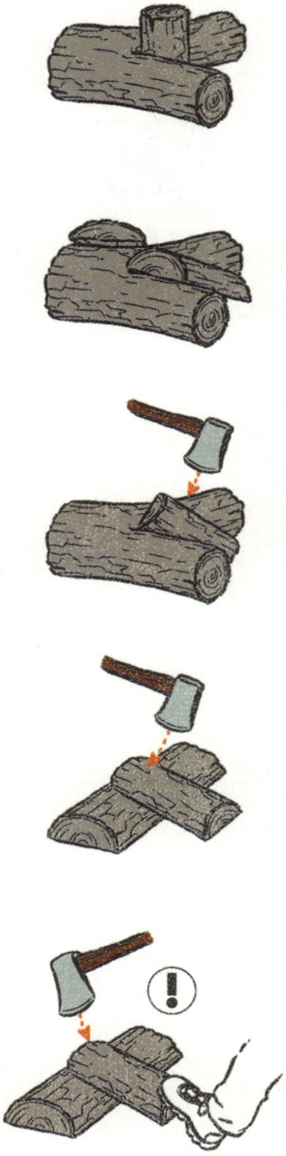

Figure 2.56

CHAPTER 2. TOOLS   51

HEWING WOOD

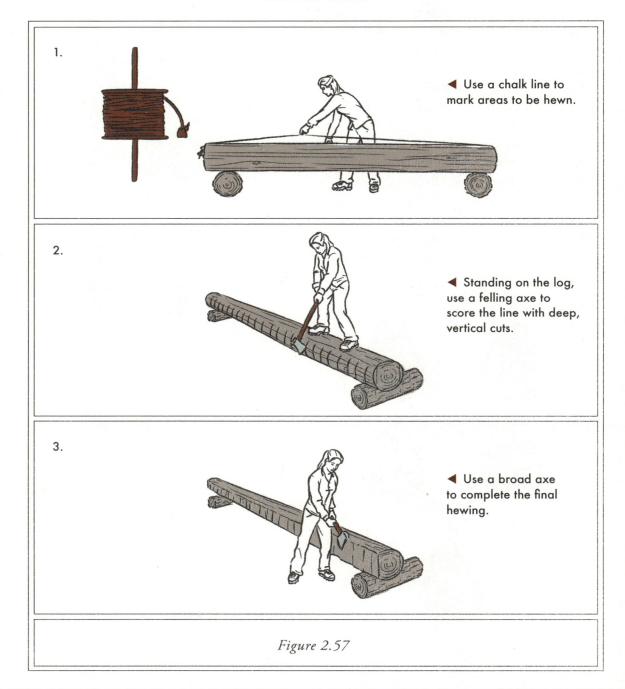

1.

◄ Use a chalk line to mark areas to be hewn.

2.

◄ Standing on the log, use a felling axe to score the line with deep, vertical cuts.

3.

◄ Use a broad axe to complete the final hewing.

Figure 2.57

Always keep safety in mind when cutting, storing, or otherwise using an axe. Here are ways to split wood safely with an anvil to stop the axe from hitting the ground and causing damage. This also helps you avoid having the axe glance out of control on a missed swing. **FIGURES 2.58 AND 2.59** show proper anvil cuts. The top illustration in **FIGURE 2.60** shows a proper anvil cut; the bottom illustration shows a wrong cut position with no safety to keep the axe from hitting the ground.

SAFE CUTTING POSITION, VERSION 1

Figure 2.58

SAFE CUTTING POSITION, VERSION 2

Figure 2.59

SAFE CUTTING POSITION VS WRONG CUTTING POSITION

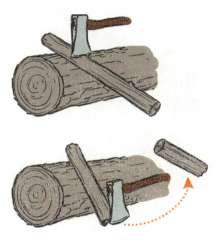

Figure 2.60

Bushcraft Tip

Never lay your axe on the ground; it could become a tripping hazard. Instead, lean it head-down against a tree or return it to your pack system.

In addition to using safe cutting practices, you need to store your axe safely as well. **FIGURE 2.61** shows a safe axe storage position.

SAFE AXE STORAGE POSITION

Figure 2.61

UNCONVENTIONAL AXE USES FOR BUSHCRAFT

Like your belt knife, the axe should be multifunctional in nature and may have to fill gaps other tools are specifically designed for should the need arise. A keen axe of the correct profile will do a very passable job as both a draw knife and a plane. See **FIGURE 2.62** for an example.

USING AN AXE AS A DRAW KNIFE AND PLANE

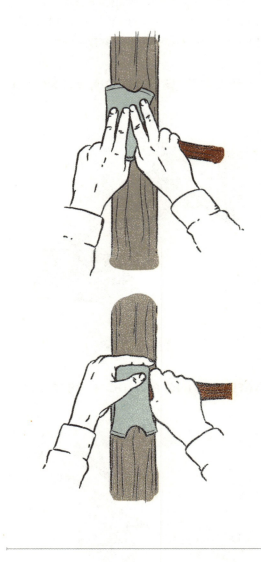

Figure 2.62

An axe head that is missing the handle can also be used effectively as a hand adze. An adze is a tool used for removing material in a controlled fashion; wood is chopped on the downswing with a perpendicular head unlike an axe. Adzes can be straight edged or curved for making gutters or concavities. This is one of the larger advantages of the tomahawk configuration as the handle is easily removable allowing the head itself to be used as a hand tool for many chores. See **FIGURE 2.63** for an example.

The axe can also be used as a chisel to remove waste from things like square notches if they are large enough by simply cutting two saw kerfs the proper dimension and then batoning the axe to remove the waste from the side. (A kerf is a slit made by a saw or the width of the cut made by a saw.) See **FIGURE 2.64** for an example of using an axe as a chisel.

AXE HEAD USED AS AN ADZE

Figure 2.63

AXE USED AS A CHISEL

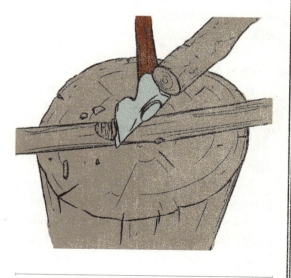

Figure 2.64

General care for the axe head and handle is the same as for the knife; however, I recommend when you first get your axe to strip any varnish or shellac the manufacturer may have added and then oil it with a boiled linseed oil or a 50-50 mix of pine tar and boiled linseed oil. At first this should be done once a day for a week, then one time a week for a month, and finally one time a month the first year. Always have a mask (sheath) for your axe and try to get only an axe or hatchet with a wooden handle in case it needs replacement.

REPLACING HANDLES

If your handle becomes loose it is most likely from drying out. Soak the axe head overnight in boiled linseed oil and it will swell the wood, making the handle become tight again.

If you break a handle and must replace it, normally you would auger into the eye to remove the wood. But if you are in the woods and have no way to do that, you can burn it out with your campfire. By placing the bit into the soil below the coals you will preserve the temper of the blade. Then only a small fire is needed around the eye to burn out the wood for handle replacement. See **FIGURE 2.65** for an example of burning out an axe handle.

BURNING OUT AN AXE HANDLE

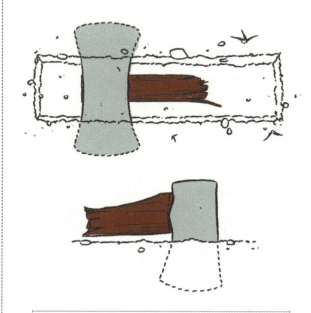

Figure 2.65

Bushcraft Tip

Caring for the head of your axe is no different than caring for any other high-carbon tool. It will rust, so it must be kept lubricated. I generally use olive oil for this purpose (although I would rarely use my axe for any food processing); it keeps things consistent in caring for all my tools and metal gear.

When replacing, be sure to have proper handle alignment, proper grain alignment, and proper axe hang. See **FIGURES 2.66 THROUGH 2.68.**

PROPER GRAIN ALIGNMENT

Good

Wedge Slot & End Grain

Bad

Figure 2.67

PROPER HANDLE ALIGNMENT

Figure 2.66

PROPER AXE HANG

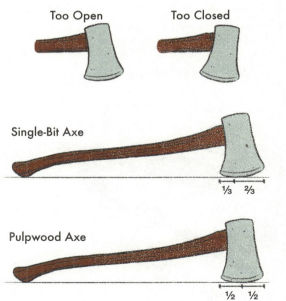

Too Open   Too Closed

Single-Bit Axe

⅓   ⅔

Pulpwood Axe

½   ½

Figure 2.68

The tools for axe maintenance are pretty simple: leather gloves, a good mill file with guard, a silicon carbide puck (a sharpening stone shaped like a puck), and some oil should keep it going for a good while in top shape. Only use a file if for some reason you have nicked the blade of your axe—or if you need to do some profile work from the onset to make it right. Other than this a puck used in circular fashion will keep the edge keen without much work. You can also use a stone similar to that used on a knife if you do not have a puck. It is a good bit of kit especially at home to have a file card for cleaning the file teeth between uses as well. See **FIGURE 2.69** for an example of an axe sharpening kit. **FIGURES 2.70 AND 2.71** show an axe sharpening puck and steps for sharpening an axe with a puck.

AXE SHARPENING PUCK

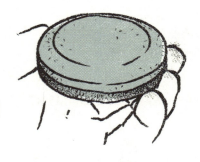

Figure 2.70

SHARPENING THE AXE WITH A PUCK

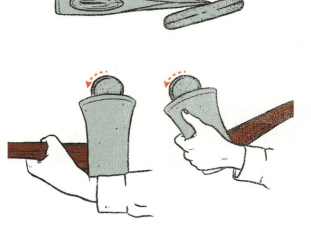

Figure 2.71

AXE SHARPENING KIT

Figure 2.69

BIT GAUGE

This gauge can be easily fashioned from wood and can later be used to ensure the same blade geometry after sharpening. See **FIGURE 2.72** for a bit gauge.

AXE GRINDS

Shown here is the proper grind for the width of the bit giving the best results. See **FIGURE 2.73** for a chart of axe grinds.

BIT GAUGE

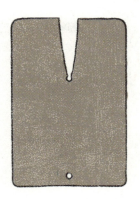

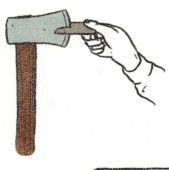

Figure 2.72

AXE GRINDS

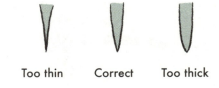

Too thin   Correct   Too thick

▲ Blunt axes glance off.   ▲ Properly sharpened axes dig in.

Figure 2.73

AXE STONE SHARPENING Similar to the knife, the axe can be sharpened by bench or field stone. When using a field stone, circular patterns like that of using the puck are recommended. See **FIGURE 2.74** for the steps to stone sharpen an axe.

AXE STONE SHARPENING

1.

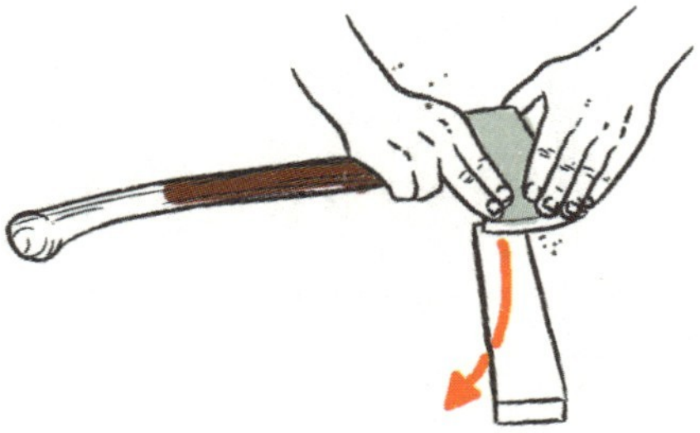

▲ Sharpen axe in a similar manner to knife.

2.

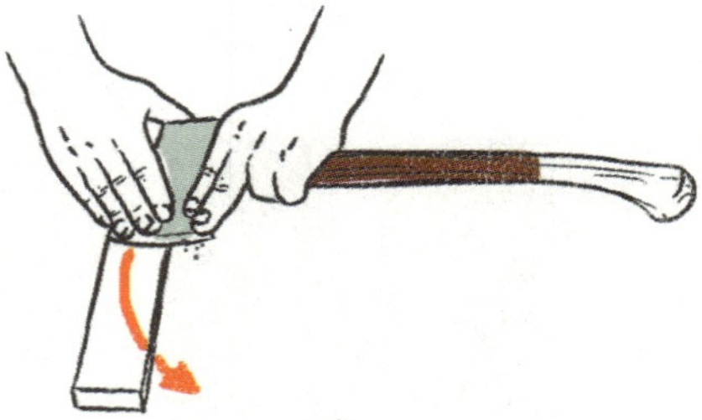

▲ Eight strokes away, eight strokes toward, eight alternate.

3.

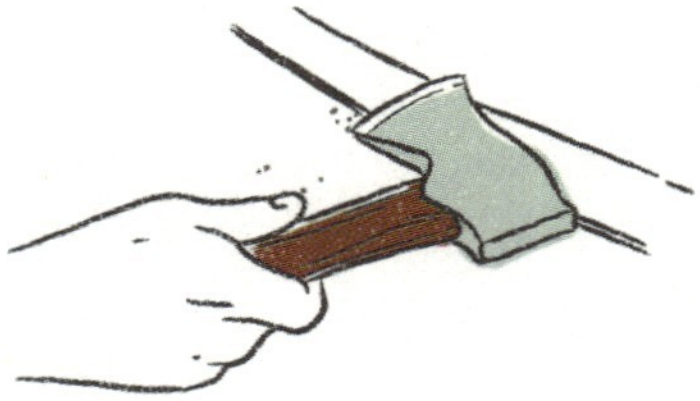

▲ Strop on a leather belt.

4.

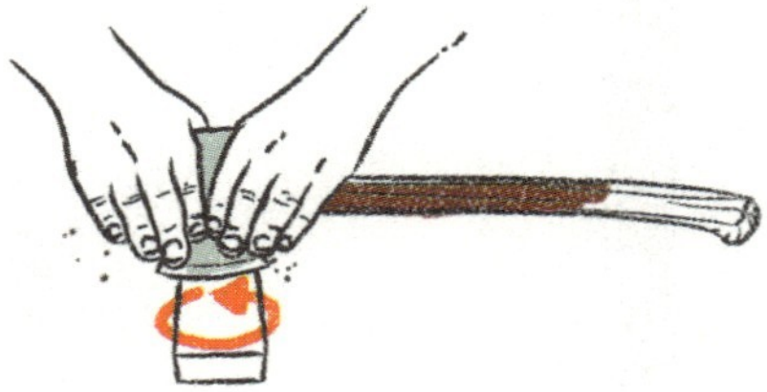

▲ In the field, use circular action on cut-down stone.

Figure 2.74

— SAWS —

Of the tools used most by bushcraft enthusiasts, the saw rounds out the top three—along with a good knife and an axe. Just like the other tools, the size and type of saw is truly dictated by its intended use. The most important things to consider when choosing a saw, besides the overall quality of the brand, are the type of blade and the TPI (teeth per inch) it has. Generally speaking you will want fewer and larger teeth for coarse work, like a pruning saw for making quick firewood. You'll want a less aggressive blade with smaller teeth and more TPI for craft work. So there is some compromise that can be made in this area.

TYPES OF SAWS

Saws come in several types and the blades are manufactured for certain tasks, depending on blade type, amount of teeth per inch, width of kerf, as well as overall tooth size. Let's look at a few different types of saws.

FOLDING SAWS

Folding saws come in many sizes, from convenient pocket carry to larger pruning-type saws. Folding saws will generally not have rakers and gullets but may have larger teeth with fewer TPI and a very wide kerf for the size of the blade. Some handsaws do have rakers and gullets, but this is rare unless you are using a very large saw of the type generally used for forestry work. There are also bucksaws that could be considered folding, but these are more often referred to as takedown models. Of the folding saws I have used, the Bahco and Silky brands are top of the line with the main difference being the bidirectional cut of the Bahco saw. Both are great for the craft in general. The advantage of the Silky brand is lots of options in saw size and TPI configurations, depending on the material you may need to process. You can find sizes up to a large 500 mm blade on the Katana Boy. See **FIGURES 2.75 THROUGH 2.77** for examples of folding saws.

SMALL FOLDING SAW

Figure 2.75

LARGER FOLDING SAW

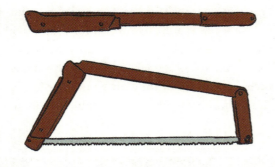

Figure 2.76

FOLDING BUCKSAW

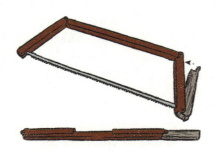

Figure 2.77

BOW SAWS/BUCKSAWS

The old school bucking and bow saws are truly a thing of the past and were generally used around the homestead for bucking, cutting the wood down to manageable size generally for later splitting for firewood. See **FIGURE 2.78** for an example of an old-fashioned bow saw.

BOW SAW FROM THE EARLY NINETEENTH CENTURY

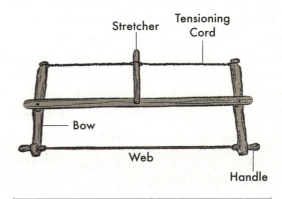

Figure 2.78

They still work well if you can find one in good shape, but in recent times they have been replaced by metal frame tubular-style saws. The advantage to the metal frame saw is, of course, durability, and the disadvantage is the difficulty to repair the frame should it be damaged. See **FIGURE 2.79** for an example of a modern bow saw.

BOW SAW

Figure 2.79

The main thing to remember with any framed saw is that the height of the frame dictates the size tree that can be cut without rolling the log. Rectangle frames are better than the triangle frames, which restrict stroke quickly. See **FIGURE 2.80** for a comparison of bow saw frames.

COMPARISON OF BOW SAW FRAMES

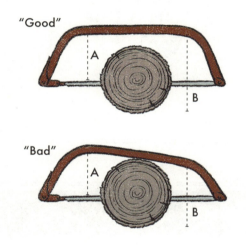

Figure 2.80

Bow saw frames are fairly easy to fashion from a green branch about 1" in diameter. It is best to use long-fibered wood for this like hickory and oak. When carrying the blade only, it helps to carry a couple of small key-ring-style split rings of about the same diameter. In place of these you can use green sticks or nails cut to length. See **FIGURES 2.81 THROUGH 2.83** for examples of bow saw frames crafted from wood.

BUSHCRAFT BOW SAW

Figure 2.81

BOW SAW FRAME WITH KEY-RING ANCHOR

Figure 2.82

CLOSE-UP OF FRAME AND BOW SAW JOINT

Figure 2.83

Another method of using the bow saw was pioneered by Swedish woodsmen to process smaller pieces of firewood. They would stand the frame upright on the ground, leaning it against the body, and holding the wood at both ends push it up and down against the blade. One has to be careful of pinching the blade with this method but after a few times getting used to it, it is a very quick method for pieces up to 2" in diameter. See **FIGURE 2.84** for an example of this style of kindling cutting with a bow saw.

SWEDISH-STYLE USE OF BOW SAW FOR CUTTING KINDLING

Figure 2.84

MAKING A WOODLAND MATERIAL BUCKSAW

Making a woodland material bucksaw is done by taking advantage of a simple machine, the windlass. You need two uprights about 15" long and about 1½" wide. The center support stick is the same width as the blade you are using and about 2" shorter. There are different joints you can use for the center support. A mortise and tenon joint (where the tenon, the peg, inserts into the mortise, the slot) will be the most secure but others will work. See **FIGURE 2.85** for an example of a mortise and tenon.

MORTISE AND TENON

Figure 2.85

A string-like paracord and a winding stick are the rest of the components needed to build the saw. Each upright will need a split for the blade and then a pin or the key ring will hold it in place when tight. It is a good idea to notch the support sticks at the top to keep the cord in place as it is wound tight with the windlass. **FIGURES 2.86 AND 2.87** show a handmade bucksaw.

HANDMADE BUCKSAW, ASSEMBLED

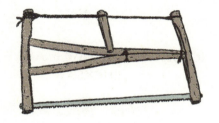

Figure 2.86

HANDMADE BUCKSAW, DISMANTLED

Figure 2.87

FIGURES 2.88 AND 2.89 show sample plans for making your own bucksaw.

PLANS FOR MAKING A BUCKSAW

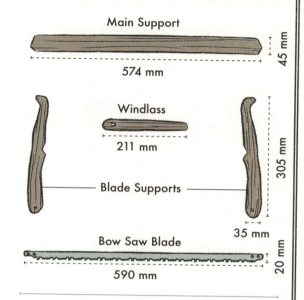

Figure 2.88

HANDMADE FOLDING BUCKSAW BY NICK STOWELL

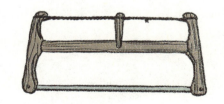

Figure 2.89

The blade's kerf is the width of the cut created by the offset of the teeth on the saw. Generally, every other tooth is bent slightly outward in opposite directions. See **FIGURE 2.90** for an example of saw kerf.

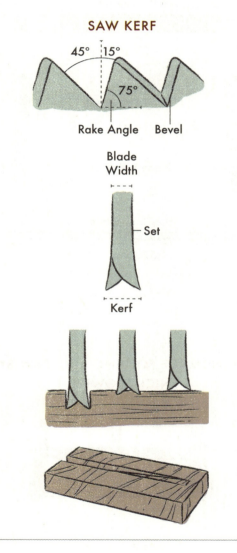

SAW KERF

45°   15°

75°

Rake Angle   Bevel

Blade Width

Set

Kerf

Figure 2.90

There are three main types of blades available for bow and bucksaw use. These are green wood (described previously in this chapter), dry wood, and bone cutting. Green wood blades involve rakers and gullets for rough cutting of green wood wet fibers and tend to be very aggressive as they have fewer TPI. In the case of bucking and bow saws they will generally include rakers and gullets to remove wood from the kerf, making them cut faster with less clogging. See **FIGURE 2.91** for an example of a green wood saw blade on a bucksaw.

GREEN WOOD SAW BLADE ON A BUCKSAW

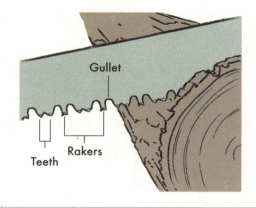

Gullet

Rakers

Teeth

Figure 2.91

The bone cutting blade is very similar to a hacksaw blade; in fact, hacksaw blades are quite often used for this purpose. A dry wood blade is absent rakers and gullets, only having staggered teeth for finer cutting on dry wood material.

One of the biggest advantages to these types of saw blades is that you can craft the saw body in the woods, only carrying the blade if that's what you choose. See **FIGURE 2.92** for an example of the difference between a green wood and a dry wood blade.

THE DIFFERENCE BETWEEN A GREEN WOOD AND A DRY WOOD BLADE

Green Wood Blade

Dry Wood Blade

Figure 2.92

Curved blades are sometimes used in both hand and folding pruning-type saws. They generally have a green wood blade and cut on only the pull strike. The curvature of the blade is designed to help in making the blade dive deeper into the wood as the cut is made.

When using any saw there are a couple of safety measures to consider. Safety glasses are always recommended. The more aggressive the saw the more chance it has to bounce a bit or jump out of the kerf when beginning the cut, so gloves are another good option. Keep your off hand completely clear of the blade. You can even reach through the frame of a buck or bow saw, crossing the cutting arm to keep a safe position. When cutting always make sure the off-fall side of the log is loose and not held in any way that is too open to the kerf as the cut is made. This will keep the saw from binding in the kerf as the cut gets deeper, actually opening the kerf to make for quicker, easier cutting. If you cannot elevate the off-fall end then cutting from the bottom up is a better option as it forces the kerf to open as you cut. This works very well with hand and folding saws. For a larger log it may be necessary to pound a wedge in to assist opening the kerf once the saw blade is below the initial cut.

Oiling the blade of the saw is a crucial part of maintaining it. Bucksaws and bow saws will almost certainly have a non-coated and carbon steel blade that will rust. Protecting the blade is another consideration if you are not using a folding or collapsible saw. An easy way to do this from natural materials is to make a rawhide slip cover that can be tied at both ends of the blade. Simply cut a piece of hide the length of the blade and about two times the width. Fold it while wet, and then pinch between a split log to dry. After this it should slide over the blade and can be tied on by wrapping cord around the blade and knotting it tight. A faster option may be to use a bark cover, if you can harvest a pliable bark like birch or even poplar. Simply cut the bark to length and bend it in half lengthwise. Then tie it to the blade.

With smaller saws like folding handsaws, any sharpening or resetting is difficult at best; for larger bow- and bucking-type blades it is a bit simpler. Generally your blade will lose kerf before dulling, giving the perception of a dull blade because it may begin to hang up in the smaller kerf. To correct this on the fly you will need a punching device like a nail and your axe. Simply lay the blade down on the flat surface of a stump and observe the teeth. The kerf is formed from the teeth being bent to one side alternating down the blade, except the raker teeth (if you have them), which will be straight. Tap each tooth

gently in the direction it was already bent (don't overdo it). Once you have done one side flip the blade and do the other. When complete, slide a sharpening stone like the ones seen earlier in this chapter (if you're carrying one) along the blade in the direction the teeth are sharpened. This will make the kerf more even and sharpen the teeth somewhat at the same time. See **FIGURE 2.93** for an example of resetting the kerf.

RESETTING THE KERF

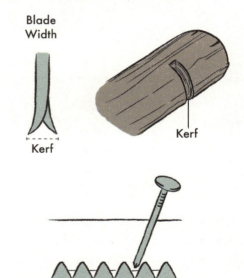

Figure 2.93

CHAPTER 3

CORDAGE AND KNOTS

YOU SHOULD CARRY cordage as one of the main elements of your kit because of its usefulness in creating other items. You should also carry it because it's difficult to create in large quantity with natural material, and doing so would take a lot of time. Cordage is useful for making fire, lashings, and bindings and is helpful in trapping, fishing, and a host of other things. Therefore, it is important for you to take a close look at the cordage you choose to carry within your kit. In this chapter you'll learn what cordage is, how to make your own cordage, how to tie knots, and how to make the best use of the cordage you carry in and that you make yourself.

— CORDAGE —

Cordage will make up one of the main elements of your kit because of its usefulness in creating other items. It is useful for making bow drill fires, lashings, and bindings and is helpful in trapping, fishing, and a host of other things. In fact, it will be used for almost everything you build in some way and in some amount. You will likely want to carry in at least some cordage, although you can make your own. See **FIGURE 3.1** for various types of cordage you may want to pack.

While using cordages you bring in is great, you will also want to think about how much you are willing to carry in as well as how you can supplement that cordage with natural materials. To do this, you need to again understand the properties of plants and trees that will produce the best materials, how to harvest these materials, and then how to fashion them into usable cord or rope depending on the task. The following list shows various types of plants that can be used for cordage.

VARIOUS TYPES OF CORDAGE

Figure 3.1

TREES
- basswood
- elm
- tulip poplar
- cedar
- aspen
- cottonwood
- hickory
- ash

STALKS
- stinging nettle
- velvet leaf
- dogbane
- milkweed
- fireweed
- hemp
- evening primrose

LEAVES
- yucca
- cattail
- bulrush

ROOTLETS
- cedar
- pine
- juniper
- tamarack
- yucca
- spruce
- sage

MISCELLANEOUS
- hair (moose, horse, etc.)
- sinew
- rawhide

TREE AND VINE CORDAGE

Trees and vines are commonly used to create cordage in the field. Vines are an easy type of natural cordage. Because I use trees for many examples in this chapter and throughout the book we should first understand the general makeup of a tree. The thing I am most fond of is that trees are a four-season resource. Many times when you are looking for a certain plant to provide tinder, cordage, or even medicine, a tree will do just as nicely. The inner bark is used for cordage. The outer bark has to come off before it can be accessed and used. The one thing to remember about trees and seasonality is that bark removal is generally much easier during the spring and early summer when the sap is running, causing a wet gap (in a sense) between the outer bark and the sapwood. See **FIGURE 3.2** for an example of a tree cross-section.

INNER BARK

Cordage material from trees is mainly harvested from the inner bark (cambium). Work with wet fibers as you can attain a tighter twist this way and the materials will be more pliable. The other advantage I find in cordage made from trees is that it does not need retting. This is a process of letting the material somewhat begin to rot, helping to separate the fibers. For many plant-based cordages, retting gives better performance but it is not needed for tree-based cordages.

The processing of the material is the key. The first thing is to separate the cambium or inner bark layer from the outer bark. This can be done by simply peeling or bending the material around a small sapling, which helps separate one from the other. See **FIGURES 3.3 AND 3.4** for examples of how to separate bark.

TREE CROSS-SECTION

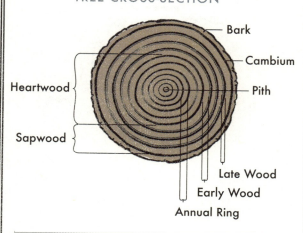

Figure 3.2

BARK SEPARATION, STEP 1

Figure 3.3

BARK SEPARATION, STEP 2

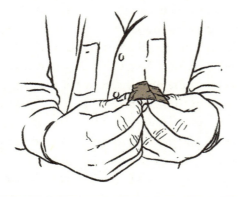

Figure 3.4

Once the inner bark has been obtained it needs to be split down further into fine fibers using the same separation method. This process will dictate how small the diameter of the cord you can make will be as well as the neatness of the finished cord. If you don't have a lot of time or you don't need very nice cordage, the raw, untwisted fibers can be used similar to a withie (discussed later in this section) for quick applications as well.

Once the fibers are obtained the cordage is made by separating them into two bundles, each half the diameter of the desired finished product. Begin by twisting both bundles in the same direction while keeping them separate. Then twist both bundles in the opposite direction together.

Note that the method of twisting a top strand only works well if you are making the cordage alone and holding the already twisted portion with one hand. If the standing end of the cord is held by a device, both strands can be twisted at the same time and then wrapped over one another in the opposite direction.

FIGURES 3.5 THROUGH 3.7 show examples of ways to twist cordage.

USING YOUR PALM TO ROLL FIBERS INTO CORDAGE

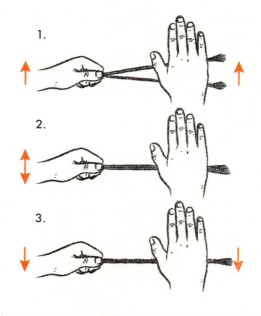

Figure 3.5

TWISTING FIBERS INTO STRONGER CORDAGE

1.

2.

3.

4.

Figure 3.6

SIMPLER TWISTING METHOD, TWISTING ONLY ONE SET OF FIBERS

1.

2.

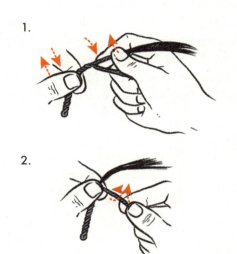

Figure 3.7

Sooner or later you will need to splice your cordage. Splicing means adding a new piece to the shorter side so the cordage can be lengthened. Do this with one end longer than the other, adding the splice to the short end one bundle at a time. This will rotate which bundle has the splice.

You can make an overlap splice just laying the bundle over the short side with a tag about 2" long and then twist as a single bundle and wrap in as you go. Or you can use a V splice that overlaps both sides and splice the new piece into both bundles at the same time. See **FIGURES 3.8 THROUGH 3.11** for examples of how to splice cordage.

Bushcraft Tip

To make a whisk find a sapling with several shoots growing from a central point. Just fold the 8" shoots backward against a 12" handle and lash them with cordage.

OVERLAP SPLICE

Figure 3.8

V SPLICE

Figure 3.10

COMPLETED EXAMPLE OF
OVERLAP SPLICE

Figure 3.9

COMPLETED EXAMPLE OF V SPLICE

Figure 3.11

WITHIES

A withie is generally considered a small willow sapling or shoot that is very flexible and can be used to tie and bind. Species like ash and hickory will also serve this purpose and a withie can also be a thin branch from these trees. Using a withie lets you avoid making cordage but still gives you a resource to use in quick lashing. Lashings are wraps of cordage used to bind components together, for things like the frame of a wigwam or to help secure other small cross poles to a structure like a lean-to. **FIGURE 3.12** shows an example of using a withie for lashing two pieces of wood together.

WITHIE USED FOR LASHING

Figure 3.12

ROOTS

Some trees will have roots that make good cord for lashing and binding as well as runners for baskets and so on. This material was used traditionally for sewing together birch bark containers. Spruce is a prime example here. You don't need to dig too deeply near the trunk to find a fairly long root runner; many are as long as 10'–20'. See **FIGURE 3.13** for an example of root runners.

ROOT RUNNERS

Figure 3.13

To use this root, remove the woody outside layer and then a supple cord will be available for use. To remove the outer material and expose the raw root, you can simply pull the root between your thumb and the spine of a good knife. If the root is thick enough, it can even be split to make two cords from one root.

When splitting roots down the middle sometimes they will tend to runoff, or get thicker on one side until the root eventually runs off the thinner side from the work piece. If this begins to happen put more bend in the root while splitting the thicker side. See **FIGURE 3.14** for an example of splitting a spruce root.

SPLITTING A SPRUCE ROOT

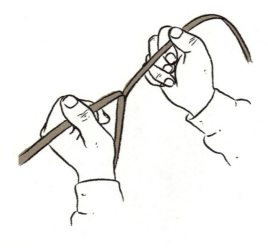

Figure 3.14

Traditionally, as seen in **FIGURE 3.15**, fire was used to help prepare spruce roots as cordage. They would hold the root over the fire until the bark peeled and then pull it through a split stick or board in the ground to remove the bark. The root would then split once and coil.

TRADITIONAL METHOD OF SPRUCE ROOT PREPARATION

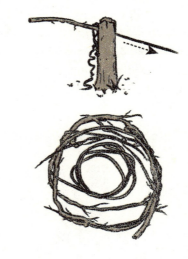

Figure 3.15

VINES

There are quite a few vines that will also make good quick cordage, like honeysuckle and Virginia creeper. Try to tie a knot in the chosen vine. If it does not break then it should be good to use. See illustrations of these plants in Chapter 10.

Most plant cordages in the Eastern Woodlands are better harvested after the first frost when the stalk has turned from green to brown (partially retted by nature). The fibers are easier to separate and remove this way. Using an anvil and baton or stone can help separate the chaff from the fibers as well. Some plants like milkweed and cattail are best harvested before the first frost as the fibers will degrade faster once dead and become more brittle.

As when working with tree bark, keeping the fibers wet while working them is important. Plant fibers can be retted in water as well by cutting and placing in a creek or stream. This must be watched carefully to catch the fibers at the prime time for harvesting. See **FIGURE 3.16** for an example of how to braid fibers together to create stronger cordage.

THREE-STRAND BRAID

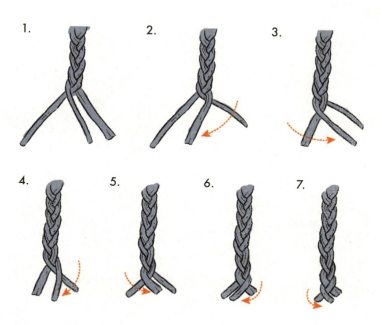

Figure 3.16

Rope can be used for many camp chores, such as suspending game animals for processing, pulling tent stakes, hanging a hammock, or improvising a windlass (see information on windlasses later in this chapter) to move a heavy object. **FIGURES 3.17a THROUGH 3.17c** show examples of rope being used for various camp chores. I recommend carrying two ropes of about 12' in length and one rope 25' in length at all times when tramping alone.

PULLING TENT STAKES

Figure 3.17b

SUSPENDING GAME

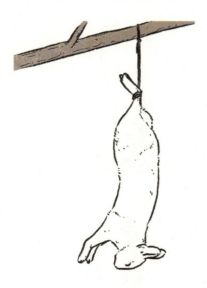

Figure 3.17a

HANGING UP A HAMMOCK

Figure 3.17c

Bushcraft Tip

Ensure that any natural cordage is not stored wet; this will cause mildew and break down the fibers.

I carry a 6' length of 550 parachute cord, aka paracord, with a bowline tied in one end and a stop knot in the other. This utility rope is useful for many things on the trail. Generally this is the first thing I use when I reach a new camp. I wrap it around a tree and place a toggle in a marline spike hitch to a desired height to hang my pack. This keeps it at a comfortable level to work out of and off the ground at the same time.

In an emergency, the rope can serve as a bow drill cord, a fast tripod lashing, and, with a barrel sling, a way to carry kindling material or wood back to camp. Doubled over I can tie simple overhand knots into it for pace counting on the trail if needed. It will make an impromptu hook for attaching a piece of gear (hatchet/carving knife) or small game to my belt, relieving my hands of the burden. It can be used in camp to attach to my carving knife sheath for neck carry while working. This is one example of the reuse for a single piece of rope.

In addition to my utility rope, I carry a ridgeline rope of approximately 25' that has a bowline loop in one end and a stop knot in the other. I generally carry a roll of #36 Mariner tarred line as well. Most other needs could be covered by withies and simple natural cordage made as needed.

Also it is important to understand gaining mechanical advantage using rope and cordage or making simple machines, so we will discuss rope tackles and the windlass as well.

See **FIGURES 3.18 TO 3.20** for an example of paracord and what you can do with it.

PARACORD

Figure 3.18

PARACORD PACK HANG

Figure 3.19

PARACORD BOW DRILL

Figure 3.20

ROPE SPINNING You can also make your own rope from natural materials. Cordage can be made larger in diameter if needed but making multiple-strand ropes and braids will make it much stronger. A three-strand rope is pretty simple to create in the woods using a simple method called the rope spinner. This requires spinning one strand of rope tight and then dividing it into thirds and spinning in the opposite direction. See **FIGURES 3.21 THROUGH 3.23** for steps on how to make rope.

ROPE SPINNING IN THREE STEPS

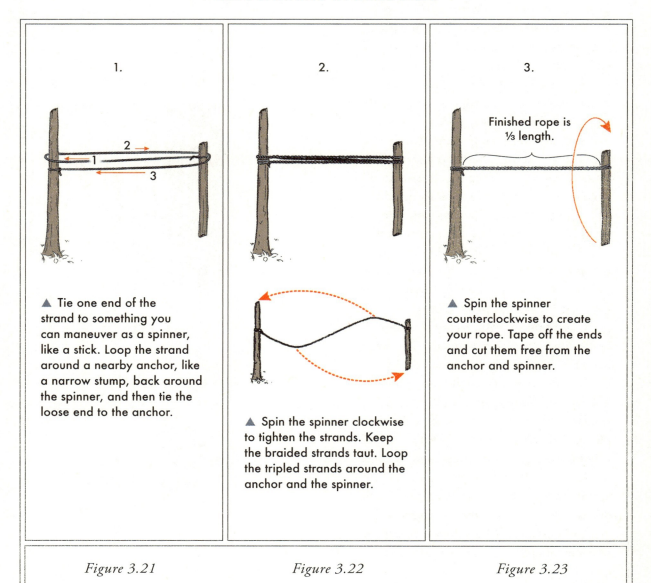

1.

▲ Tie one end of the strand to something you can maneuver as a spinner, like a stick. Loop the strand around a nearby anchor, like a narrow stump, back around the spinner, and then tie the loose end to the anchor.

2.

▲ Spin the spinner clockwise to tighten the strands. Keep the braided strands taut. Loop the tripled strands around the anchor and the spinner.

3.

Finished rope is ⅓ length.

▲ Spin the spinner counterclockwise to create your rope. Tape off the ends and cut them free from the anchor and spinner.

Figure 3.21   *Figure 3.22*   *Figure 3.23*

— LASHINGS —

Lashings are used when making objects that need to take strain. They are made through a series of wraps and fraps with the cordage or rope. Tripods, pack frames, camp furniture, and A-frame shelter supports all require lashings to make them strong. For basic bushcraft, you need to know how to use the straight or shear lash and the diagonal or cross lash. Shear lashings are used when two objects are tied side by side and then separated, causing the lashing to tighten further. A diagonal lash is used with sticks that cross each other while being lashed. See **FIGURES 3.24 THROUGH 3.26** for examples of these lashings.

SHEAR LASHING, STEP-BY-STEP

SHEAR LASHING, CLOSE-UP

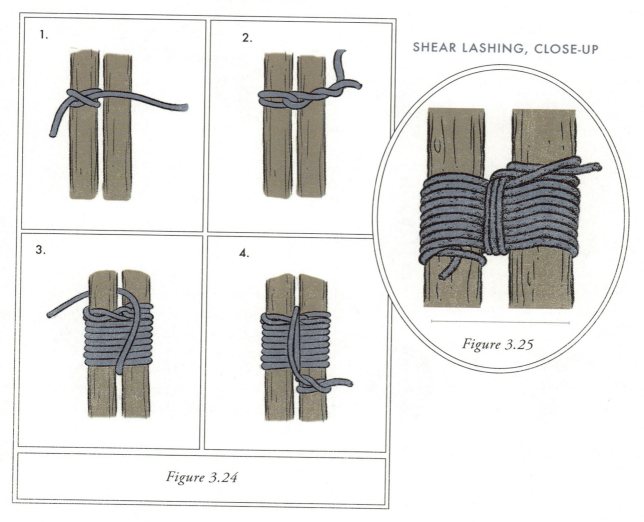

Figure 3.25

Figure 3.24

DIAGONAL LASHING

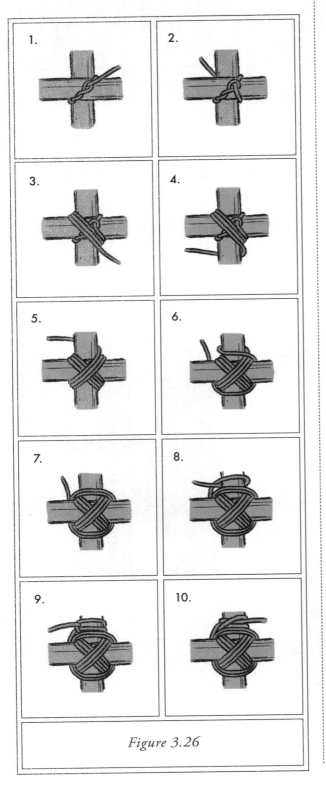

Figure 3.26

Other lashings that you may find helpful are continuous lashing, which helps when building around camp, and square lashing, which helps secure two things at right angles. See **FIGURES 3.27 AND 3.28** for examples.

CONTINUOUS LASHING

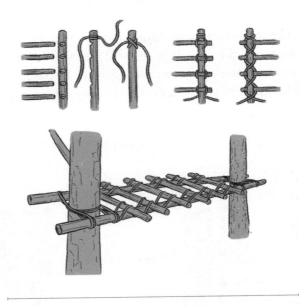

Figure 3.27

Bushcraft Tip

Whether you're tying down gear to a frame or building a shelter, the use of knots, lashings, and bindings is a critical skill. Proper lashings can mean the difference in a shelter that stands a storm or one that collapses under the weight of snow, and a pack frame that lasts for years or breaks three miles into a weekend tramp.

SQUARE LASHING

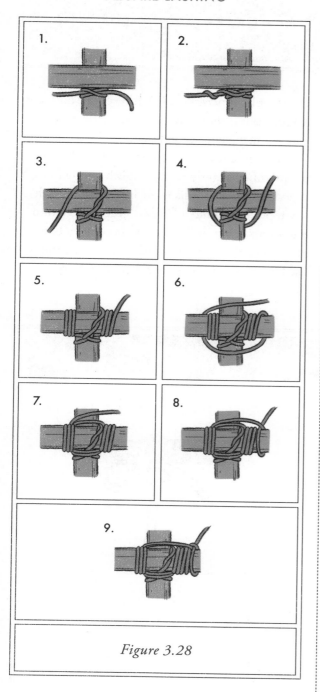

Figure 3.28

TRIPOD LASHING

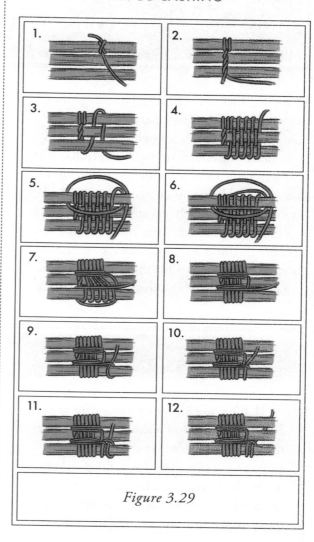

Figure 3.29

TRIPOD LASHING ON ROPE STOOL

Figure 3.30

Tripod lashing requires a more complex series of turns. See **FIGURE 3.29** for an example of tripod lashing. Tripod lashing is useful for constructing camp furniture as seen in **FIGURE 3.30**.

━ KNOTS AND HITCHES ━

When it comes to the bushcrafter using knots (which tie two ropes together or one end of a rope to itself) and hitches (which tie a rope to some other object), it's important to realize that, although there are many different types, knowing just a few will help you do many things. The key is to understand which few are the best to know. You can attempt to learn the 100-plus knots available or you can find the ones most multifunctional for your needs. One thing I try to teach is that if at all possible cordage should be easily recoverable. If necessary, it can be cut to different lengths, but it should be reusable many times without being cut beyond that.

Many hitches can be combined in use or simply modified slightly to accomplish another task. A good example of this is the lark's head, which when placed around a larger object in a continuous loop like a bundle of wood becomes a barrel hitch or girth hitch—essentially that same thing used in a different manner for another purpose.

HALF HITCHES

Half hitches are quick knots with many functions, including making fast tools, like the half-hitch ladder, on the fly. They are also well suited to combine with other knots using a bight to tie the hitch, allowing for quick release. See **FIGURES 3.31 AND 3.32** for examples of a slippery half-hitch knot.

SLIPPERY HALF HITCH, COMPLETED

Figure 3.32

SLIPPERY HALF HITCH, STEP 1

Figure 3.31

MARLINE SPIKE HITCH

The marline spike hitch is one of my personal favorites. I feel it is the most versatile of them all when it comes to accomplishing basic camp makings. It can secure a hammock, hang a pack, secure a tarp (by using it on stakes), hang gear from ridgelines on a toggle, hang a pot with a toggle on your tripod, and even make a rope ladder if you are so inclined. **FIGURE 3.33** shows the marline spike hitch.

MARLINE SPIKE HITCH

Figure 3.33

Bushcraft Tip

The timber hitch is great to use when creating a ridgeline for a shelter.

TIMBER HITCH

This is a friction loop that is used to start most lashings and because it is actually only a friction of the bight itself against an object like a pole, there is nothing to untie when recovering the cordage at this end. It can also be used for bow strings and for slippery hitches around objects like trees. See **FIGURE 3.34** for an example of a timber hitch and **FIGURE 3.35** for an example of a timber hitch with a half hitch.

TIMBER HITCH

Figure 3.34

TIMBER HITCH WITH HALF HITCH

Figure 3.35

CLOVE HITCH

The clove hitch is an ending hitch mainly used for lashings (from my perspective). However, it can be used to finish any wrapping for camp projects like hooks for hanging pots over a fire from a galley pole. See **FIGURE 3.36** for an example of a clove hitch.

CLOVE HITCH

Figure 3.36

Bushcraft Tip

The clove hitch is very useful if you need to adjust the line after setting. The knot will loosen when either end of the rope is pushed toward the knot. It is a good ending knot for lashings, as it makes cord recovery possible.

KLEMHEIST KNOT

This is a great alternative for tightening tarps and holding tension on a ridgeline. It can also be used on rope as a safety loop when using rope bridges. See **FIGURE 3.37** for an example of tying a klemheist knot. See **FIGURE 3.38** for an example of a completed klemheist knot.

TYING A KLEMHEIST KNOT

Figure 3.37

COMPLETED KLEMHEIST KNOT

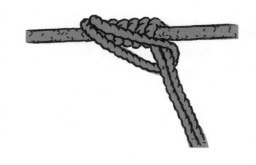

Figure 3.38

The barrel sling is a simple knot that can be used for many applications, from simple toggle attachment to lifting and carrying objects. Variations of this knot (the lark's head hitch and girth hitch) can be used for more permanent attachment of toggles, and also for single lines used with marline spikes. See **FIGURE 3.39** for an example of a barrel sling, **FIGURE 3.40** for an example of a lark's head used to create a toggle, and **FIGURE 3.41** for an example of a girth hitch.

BARREL SLING

Figure 3.39

LARK'S HEAD USED TO CREATE A TOGGLE

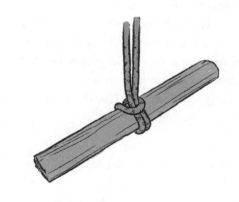

Figure 3.40

GIRTH HITCH

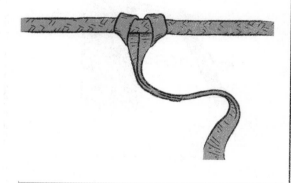

Figure 3.41

HALF-HITCH LADDER

This knot is great to secure blanket roll setups and rolled canvas-like tents. It can also be used to secure a sail to a mast, or simply combined with a timber hitch to drag a log. It also works exceptionally well for simple rope ladders that are made from a single length of cord or rope and the rung materials. See **FIGURE 3.42** for an example of a half-hitch ladder.

HALF-HITCH LADDER

Figure 3.42

TRUCKER'S HITCH

The trucker's hitch has been used by farmers and load carriers for many moons. It has been used as a standard called the rope tackle by the Boy Scouts for tensioning ropes on all kinds of pioneering-type projects. It works very well for securing and tightening a tarp ridgeline. With one end of the rope already tied off, tie a slippery half hitch in the bight, make a wrap around your other fixed point, feed the free end through the loop, and then lock off with another slippery hitch. When combined with a rolling hitch it will hold fairly solid on its own to allow security hitches without pinching tension. This works well for ridgelines as well as bedrolls. See **FIGURE 3.43** for an example of a trucker's hitch.

TRUCKER'S HITCH

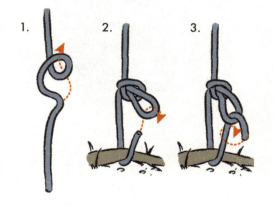

Figure 3.43

ARBOR KNOT

This knot has been generally used for securing line to a cylinder, like a spool or fishing reel, but can easily be used to secure compressible objects like blankets and tents. Because it employs a tag with a stop knot, it will not slip under tension unless the tag end is used to loosen the knot. It has also been called the Canadian jam knot when used for these purposes. To tie an arbor knot, bring the running end around your cylinder and tie an overhand knot around the standing part. Make another overhand knot, close to the first, and cut the end so it's fairly short. This will keep the end of the tie from getting mixed up with the rest of your rope or cordage as it is wound around the cylinder. See **FIGURE 3.44** for an example of an arbor knot.

ARBOR KNOT

Figure 3.44

BOWLINE KNOT

The bowline knot is used to create a loop on the end of a line. This knot is easy to undo even if the loop has been under tension, which makes it ideal to conserve cord and rope. See **FIGURE 3.45** for an example of how to tie a bowline knot.

BOWLINE KNOT

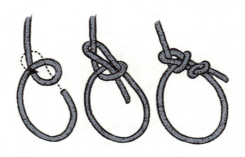

Figure 3.45

Bushcraft Tip

The single downside of the bowline knot is its tendency to slide or come undone under a heavy load, depending on the cord used to make it. However, this can be easily circumvented with a stop knot—a simple overhand knot used at the end of a line that will keep the rope from slipping—tied on the tail.

SQUARE KNOT

The square knot is used to connect lines together as well as tie off cordage with a nonslip knot. Again this knot is fairly easily untied even if tension has been applied, making it good for many applications. I even use it daily to tie my boots, tucking the tag ends inside. To tie a square knot, make a crossing turn, then bring the running end up through it, and then behind the standing part. Twist the running end all the way around the standing part and back down through the crossing turn. Take out all the slack to make the loop secure. As you tighten the knot, make sure you pull on all the leads. You can also tie the bowline loop with an extra hitch, especially if you want to increase security. See **FIGURE 3.46** for an example of a square knot.

SQUARE KNOT

Figure 3.46

DOUBLE FISHERMAN'S KNOT

A continuous loop is best made with a double fisherman's knot from a single piece of rope about 12" long, unless you are using your (longer) utility rope to carry wood. I carry generally four to six of these loops made from #36 Mariner line. Two of these left on your ridgeline will make for quick setups with a tarp in changing weather. To tie a double fisherman's knot, lay the two ends of the ropes parallel to each other and tie a double overhand knot on each of the two sides. Tighten up each double overhand knot and pull the two ropes apart so that they form a circle. See **FIGURE 3.47** for an example of a double fisherman's knot.

DOUBLE FISHERMAN'S KNOT

Figure 3.47

Bushcraft Tip

A fisherman's knot is also a slipknot and tightens against the opposite knot when pulled. However, it can be loosened easily by pulling on the tails.

ALPINE BUTTERFLY KNOT

This knot is ideal for creating continuous loops. It is strong and will hold under tension. To tie an alpine butterfly knot twist the rope twice to make two adjacent crossing turns. Pull down the outer turn. Bring the middle of the loop up through the center of the other crossing turn. To tighten the loop, pull on all the leads. See **FIGURE 3.48** for an example of an alpine butterfly knot.

ALPINE BUTTERFLY KNOT

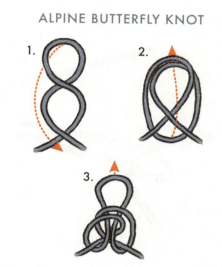

Figure 3.48

KNOTS AND HITCHES IN ACTION

When constructing almost anything from the landscape, be it a ladder, a bow drill, or a shelter, some cordage will be required and a way to secure it is a simple hitch, knot, or lashing. I truly believe that even though a little goes a long way this may be one of the most overlooked of skill sets along with making simple cordages and withies to conserve cordage when we can. **FIGURES 3.49 THROUGH 3.52** show examples of the knots and hitches in action.

ROPE TACKLE

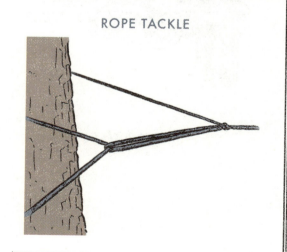

Figure 3.49

ROUND TURN IN A ROPE TACKLE

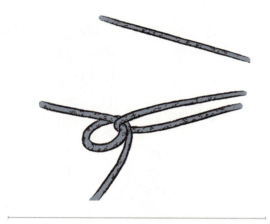

Figure 3.50

ROUND TURN

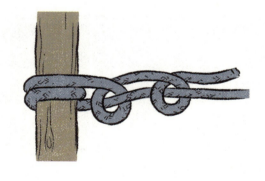

Figure 3.51

ROPE TACKLE WITH A SLIPPERY HITCH

Figure 3.52

PULLEY CONFIGURATIONS

When ropes are combined with pulleys, you can lift heavier objects by use of block-and-tackle systems. This is especially useful when you're constructing shelters, hanging game, or moving large logs. See **FIGURE 3.53** for an example of pulley configuration you can use to lift and drag heavy objects.

WOODEN PULLEYS

Figure 3.53

WINDLASS

The windlass is one of the most amazing of simple machines. It has a great variety of uses including creating tourniquets and trap engines, and its versatility is hard to match when it comes to bushcraft. I have spent years trying out different methods for accomplishing camp tasks and the windlass is at the top of my list as something simple requiring only a few components. See **FIGURES 3.54 THROUGH 3.61** for examples of using knots to create windlasses.

SPANISH WINDLASS FOR BENDING WOOD

Figure 3.54

WINDLASS FOR MOVING HEAVY OBJECTS

Figure 3.55

FLIP-FLOP WINCH, STEP 1

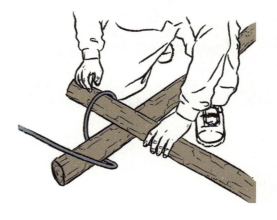

Figure 3.56

FLIP-FLOP WINCH, STEP 2

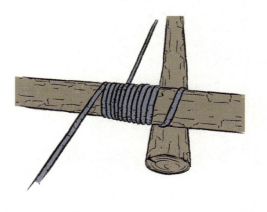

Figure 3.57

BUCKSAW

Figure 3.58

WINDLASS USED IN A TRAP

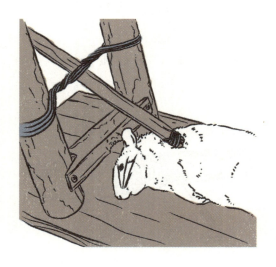

Figure 3.59

WINDLASS FENCING

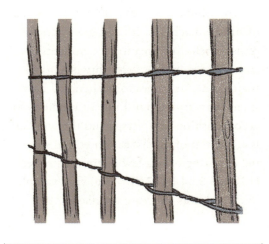

Figure 3.60

WINDLASS TOURNIQUET

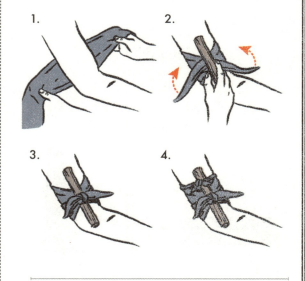

Figure 3.61

CHAPTER 4

CONTAINERS AND COOKING TOOLS

WHEN YOU'RE OUT in the woods you'll need the right tools for heating water, cooking foods, and making medicinal teas and decoctions (as discussed in Chapter 11). You'll want to choose bottles, cups, pots, and pans that are made from the right material, which depends on your needs in the bush. For example, if you're able to pack heavy items in, then the old standby of cast iron is a good choice. But for the woodsman trying to travel light and live off the land, lighter-weight materials are preferable. Steel, stainless steel, and anodized aluminum are all passable choices, depending on your personal taste and preference, but stainless steel is the winner for sheer durability. In this chapter you'll learn everything you need to know about what to bring into the woods and how to use what you bring.

WATER BOTTLES/CANTEENS

Containers are crucial to any kit; you'll find it difficult to make a container for water from natural materials. Carrying in a container is especially important because you will need to be able to disinfect water by filtering it and then heating it. You may be able to carry water in a bark container, for example, but you wouldn't be able to boil water in it. Any container you carry must be capable of withstanding direct flame. I recommend a stainless steel water bottle that holds at least 32 ounces. **FIGURE 4.1** shows an example of a water bottle that will do well in the wild.

STAINLESS STEEL WATER BOTTLE

Figure 4.1

POTS

Bush pots and cook sets sometimes nest so that several pieces can be carried in one space within the pack. There are many types of bush pots and cook sets available. See **FIGURES 4.2 THROUGH 4.8** for examples.

Bushcraft Tip

If you're using cast iron, be sure it's seasoned. This means the pores of the iron are saturated with oil and grease, making the cookware nonstick and adding to the flavor of the food cooked in it.

BUSH POT

Figure 4.2

LIDDED BUSH POT

Figure 4.3

CANTEEN AND COOK SET

Figure 4.4

SWEDISH COOK SET

Figure 4.5

TRANGIA COOK SET

Figure 4.6

TRAIL PRO COOK SET

Figure 4.7

COOK SET WITH SKILLET

Figure 4.8

The most useful way to hang a bush pot over a fire for cooking or water heating is the tripod and the crane with an adjustable pot hanger (also called a pot hook). Keep cooking utensils like a meat fork within reach.

TRIPODS

Tripods are made by shear lashing three sticks of equal length, about 1½"–2" in diameter (see the description of shear lashing in Chapter 3). These sticks should be wedged or pointed on the non-lashed end to help keep them from slipping on wet ground or snow. Lash a toggle to the line using a V notch and a clove hitch knot, or a marline spike hitch. You can adjust the height by small amounts and move the legs of the tripod from side to side to control the distance of the pot from the flames. *Don't fuss with the cordage or pot while you're moving the tripod.* See **FIGURE 4.9** for an example of a tripod.

TRIPOD

To Tripod Is
Shear-Lashed,
Leaving a Tail to
Attach a Toggle

To Tripod

Toggle
Is Longer
Than Bail
Span

Figure 4.9

CRANES

A crane is a simple machine that will help you raise and lower, or otherwise position, your pot over the fire. The most basic crane involves a stick and fork. The long stick is sharpened on one end and notched with a log cabin notch on the other. Drive the point of the long stick into the soil, then place a stick with a Y fork underneath to hold the stick in place. These pieces can be adjusted to increase or decrease the angle raising or lowering the pot. The pot is suspended by the bail from the log cabin notch, which keeps it from slipping down the stick. See **FIGURE 4.10** for an example of a simple pot crane.

SIMPLE POT CRANE

Figure 4.10

A slightly more complicated pot crane has two Y fork sticks holding it up. This is a bit more stable. See **FIGURE 4.11** for an example.

HORIZONTAL POT CRANE

Figure 4.11

POT HANGERS

A pot hanger is exactly what it sounds like—a hook or upside-down fork, notched piece of wood, or combined pieces of wood that are notched and lashed to suspend your pot over your fire. Pot hangers can be carved from wood and attached to the tripod, galley pole, or crane to hold the pot. See **FIGURES 4.12 AND 4.13** for examples of pot hangers.

POT HANGERS

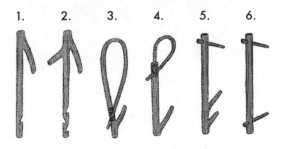

Figure 4.12

POT HANGERS IN USE

Figure 4.13

MEAT FORK

You can fashion a simple fork for cooking meat from a stick. This will help you move the meat around while cooking. See **FIGURE 4.14** for an example.

MEAT FORK

Figure 4.14

— STOVES —

In bushcraft, a stove is the stand, grated material, or component on which the pot or cup rests over the burner. It is used to raise the pot or cup being heated above the flames of the fire to provide space between the fire and the bottom of the object, allowing oxygen flow. There are many small folding versions of these stands available. See **FIGURES 4.15 THROUGH 4.17** for examples of stove stands.

FOLDING STOVE

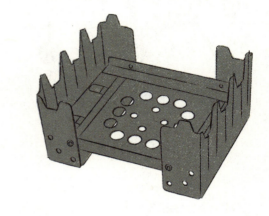

Figure 4.16

BACKPACKING STOVE

Figure 4.15

SINGLE BURNER STOVE

Figure 4.17

COOKING FIRE ARRANGEMENTS

You can use natural materials to craft grills, contain a fire, and cook your meals. **FIGURES 4.18 THROUGH 4.23** show examples of some of these arrangements.

WOODCRAFT GRILLS

Figure 4.18

▲ Used for cooking like a rack over the fire; they're usually made of green wood to inhibit burning.

DAKOTA FIRE HOLE

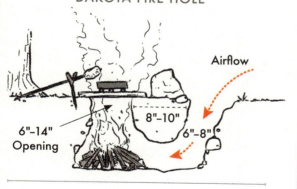

Figure 4.19

▲ Generally used in areas of fire danger, or used to conserve wood as they are very fuel efficient.

OPEN TRENCH FIREPLACE

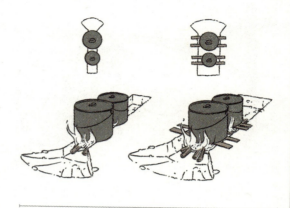

Figure 4.20

▲ Takes advantage of cross breeze to feed the fire with air, but allows for a larger fire to use more cooking implements at the same time.

PIT BAKING

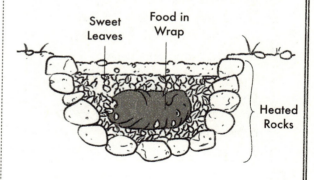

Figure 4.21

▲ When pit baking you are essentially turning a hole in the ground into an oven.

U WALL FIREPLACE WITH POT CRANE

Figure 4.22

▲ A fire wall is basically a thermal mass heat collector and can help to block wind and radiate heat; sometimes a pot crane is used in conjunction with this type of arrangement.

Bushcraft Tip

Any stones used for cooking or placed directly within a fire should never come from creek beds or rivers. Even if they appear dry, they can still hold moisture that will cause a fracture when heated; they can create great danger from flying debris when they explode.

REFLECTOR BAKING

Figure 4.23

▲ With reflector baking you are making use of a metal box with a shelf to convective cook something by the radiant heat of the fire.

CHAPTER 5

CAMP CRAFT

CAMP CRAFT IS the part of bushcraft that most people understand pretty well. It involves making usable objects from the surrounding area so you don't have to carry as many things into the woods in your pack. It could be as simple as a pot crane for cooking or a spatula for turning the Johnny cakes or as complicated as shelter and furniture building. Camp craft is only dictated by your own skill level and availability of usable resources.

When setting up camp, you'll need to consider the resources you may need to complete your tasks. For example, it may not be enough to have plenty of down and dead wood for fire building if you need structural sapling material for a raised bed or shelter framing. Also, things like a good spot to fish the bank or a good stand on hickory for squirrel hunting may be of concern when selecting an area. In this chapter, you'll learn how to create shelter, hammocks, and even camp furniture from natural materials.

CAMP SHELTER

Choosing proper shelter or coverage for your journey into the wild depends on the type of environment you'll be entering, the season, and how long you'll be staying. Obviously a weekend in warm weather doesn't require as much gear as a week-long stay in winter months.

TARPS AND TARP TENTS

The biggest advantage of the tarp or tarp tent is that it provides a no-floor footprint. A waterproof floor can trap water, creating dampness and condensation. Another advantage is that tarps and tarp tents are easy to carry and pack. They are also the most versatile and can be set up differently depending on weather and season. The most common materials for these items are polypropylene, silnylon (silicone-impregnated nylon), canvas, or oilcloth.

Each type has distinct advantages and disadvantages. Weight, durability, and ease of repair are key factors. I prefer heavier material like oilcloth in the winter and lighter nylons in the summer.

MAKING A CANVAS TENT

You can make a simple tarp tent from any painter's-type canvas drop cloth. A size of 9' × 12' will give a good number of options for setup, and it can be treated easily with products such as Kiwi Camp Dry or Thompson's WaterSeal to create a tough water barrier. You will need tie-out points on this canvas for driving stakes and running guy lines. Lay the tarp out on the ground; for each corner, take a marble, stone, or wad of leaves and bunch the fabric around this object, tying it off and leaving tails to form a loop. You will want one of these in each corner to start. After this is accomplished, fold the tarp lengthwise, and again make loops, not only at the corners but at the center as well, evenly spaced between the corner and center. Then, fold the tarp the opposite length, doing the same step as before, including the marble, stone, or bunch of leaves, adding a loop at each corner and at each side of the center, evenly spaced. Once this is complete, fold the tarp at its widest point halfway to center from both ends, and again make tie-outs on the corners. You should now have a number of tie-outs for making several different setups easily. See **FIGURES 5.1 THROUGH 5.3** for examples of tarp tie-outs and configurations.

TARP TIE-OUTS

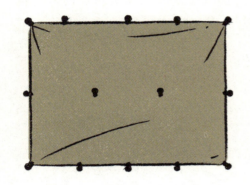

Figure 5.1

SQUARE TARP PLOW POINT

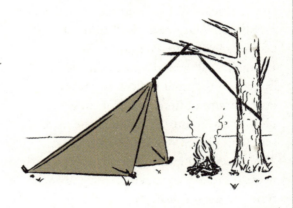

Figure 5.2

TARP TENT SETUP

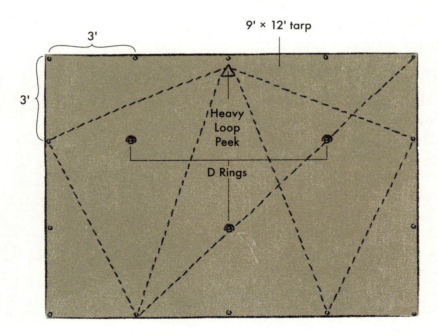

9' × 12' tarp

3'

3'

Heavy
Loop
Peek

D Rings

Figure 5.3

Even if you don't have a tarp or a tent, you can create shelter from the natural surroundings. Your first consideration should be the type of material available in the area. Using deadfall material creates the least impact on the environment and takes the least amount of time and effort to gather. However, you must ensure that the materials (and the shelter) are structurally safe. Though the materials are dead, they may need to support considerable weight by the time you are finished. Any main supports (which should be at least 3" in diameter—about the size of your wrist, or three fingers wide) should be cut green, if at all possible. External framework not supporting total weight can be constructed from dead fallen material with little risk. Following are examples of natural shelters you can build.

LEAN-TO

If the weather is okay and you can take advantage of the breeze, a lean-to–style shelter is best. You can make a lean-to by lashing a simple cross pole between trees. Add several more saplings at a 45-degree angle to the ground on one side, then weave in horizontal vines or cuttings. Once this is accomplished, waterproof the lean-to by adding more cuttings from bottom to top, layering them always with the growth upside down. (This will allow water to be channeled away from the shelter. If any cuttings are placed as they grow, water will collect toward the joints and run down into the shelter.) Avoid branches that can catch water or rain and drip inside the shelter. See **FIGURES 5.4 AND 5.5** for examples of lean-to shelters.

LEAN-TO WITH FIRE BACKER

Figure 5.4

CLOSED SIDE LEAN-TO

Figure 5.5

A-FRAME

For worse weather—stormy or colder—build another side opposite to the first side on the lean-to shelter, creating an A-frame. This deflects rain or wind from two sides. Again, don't leave any branches or supports from the inside sticking out, or the shelter will collect water. The colder the weather, the thicker the thatching must be. **FIGURES 5.6 THROUGH 5.10** show examples of A-frame lean-tos.

MAKING AN A-FRAME

Figure 5.6

RAISED BED LEAN-TO USING A TARP

Figure 5.7

RAISED BED ROPE A-FRAME

Figure 5.8

OPEN A-FRAME WITH A FIRE

Figure 5.9

A-FRAME WITH A CANVAS SLEEVE

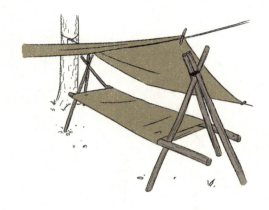

Figure 5.10

DEBRIS HUT FRAME

Figure 5.11

DEBRIS HUT

If it's very cold, a debris hut can keep you warm. A debris hut is a modification of the A-frame, with one end of the ridgepole on the ground, creating a closed triangle structure with a small opening. Debris huts work best if they are kept very small. They only need to be large enough to accommodate your body. Restricting the amount of space allows you to trap the warmth from your body inside the hut.

A bedding of leaves and debris on the ground of any shelter should be at least 4" thick when compressed to avoid coldness and wetness on the ground from seeping through. Once you're inside the debris hut, you can use your pack to close the opening behind you. **FIGURE 5.11** shows a debris hut frame. **FIGURE 5.12** shows a debris hut partially completed.

PARTIALLY COMPLETE DEBRIS HUT

Figure 5.12

— SLEEPING OPTIONS —

Once you've made a shelter you need to figure out where you'll sleep and what you'll sleep on. Here are some suggestions on things you should know about hammocks and bedrolls.

HAMMOCKS

Hammocks keep you off the ground and away from most critters. They are lightweight, easy to pack, quick to set up, and relatively easy to keep dry. Most modern hammocks are made from nylon-type parachute materials, but they can be made from rope as well as canvas. See **FIGURES 5.13 THROUGH 5.15** for examples of types of hammocks.

CANVAS HAMMOCK

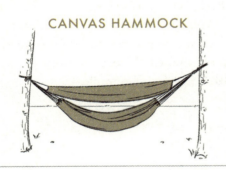

Figure 5.13

NET HAMMOCK

Figure 5.14

ROPE HAMMOCK

Figure 5.15

Most modern hammocks are tied off between two trees, using either heavy rope or strapping material such as nylon webbing. Most come equipped with carabiner clips that you clip to the straps. Add a tarp above the hammock to keep rain off. You can use hammocks in colder environments or seasons, but special care must be taken to avoid convection because of the risk of hypothermia. Hang a thick sleeping pad or underquilt below the hammock. This will trap air between the hammock and the quilt but not allow convective breezes to touch the bottom of the hammock that is against your body. You can also use a sleeping bag or wool blanket with the hammock in colder weather. See **FIGURES 5.16 AND 5.17** for summer and winter hammock setups.

SUMMER HAMMOCK SETUP

Figure 5.16

WINTER HAMMOCK SETUP WITH UNDERQUILT

Figure 5.17

You can also hang your hammock from tripods that you lash together with cordage. See **FIGURE 5.18**.

HAMMOCK ON TRIPODS

Figure 5.18

RAISED PLATFORMS

If you don't want to use a hammock, another way to get your bed off the ground is to use a raised platform for sleeping. See **FIGURE 5.19** for an example.

RAISED SLEEPING PLATFORM

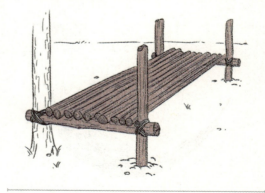

Figure 5.19

In the interest of bushcraft and the use of natural materials, I hesitate to speak much to the new synthetic material sleeping bags. They are certainly warm if you purchase the proper brand, but for the sake of staying closer to the natural world this section concentrates on how to construct and carry an old-fashioned bedroll, which is a combination of your total sleep system rolled into one unit, utilizing things like canvas, oilcloth, and wools.

Author and woodsman Horace Kephart said that it is better to carry two thin wool blankets than one thicker one. Trapped air between the blankets does not allow the heat to flow through and escape. First, let's speak to the use of the two thin wool blankets. Two wool blankets can be used individually, folded over like a sleeping bag, doubled up or pinned together to form a larger envelope. One could be folded and pinned to use as a bed sack, by stuffing with materials that will insulate, and then the other as a top quilt in colder weather. You could also overlap them in halves on a diamond to swaddle in the same fashion as a larger blanket to increase air space trapped in layers.

BED SACK

You can create a bed sack with the two thin wool blankets. You can opt to pin the bed sack together with something like horse blanket pins (very handy bit of kit) or just leave it folded in case you want to pull out one blanket quickly in the morning for sitting around the fire. This configuration is really designed to work with a groundsheet and some browse or other padding below to battle conduction (equalization of ground temperature to the body, causing heat loss), so don't forget that part in case you decide it is easier or more convenient to carry a sleep pad as well (although not very natural).

GROUNDSHEET

The groundsheet is an integral part of this system for sleeping especially if you plan to sleep on the ground. It can be a rubberized (gum) blanket like the ones used in the Civil War that are basically a piece of canvas painted with liquid rubber. These are a bit heavy by comparison for the size but dandy as a direct groundsheet. One could also use a canvas or oilcloth tarp as part of this system for the ground cloth.

GROUND PADS

Ground pads eliminate conductive cooling from the ground by keeping your body from direct contact. There are many commercial ground pads on the market made from a variety of materials. Blow-up mattresses are prone to punctures, although they will fold up smaller than a foam pad. However, a foam pad is very resistant to tearing from sticks and roots, and is easy to dry when the ground is moist. I prefer an exercise mat from a local box store; my mat is black, so it absorbs heat. Any ground pad must be thick enough when compressed to battle the effects of conduction and yet be manageable for carry outside the pack.

ROLLING A BEDROLL, VERSION 1

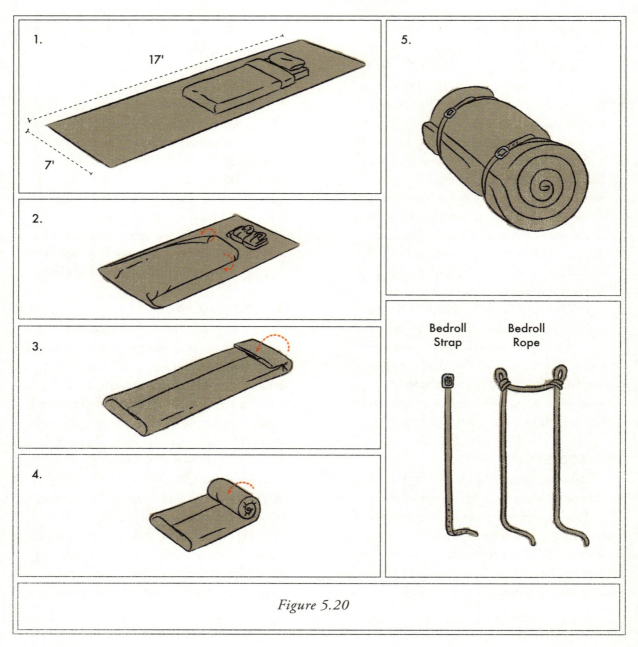

1.

17'

7'

2.

3.

4.

5.

Bedroll
Strap

Bedroll
Rope

Figure 5.20

ROLLING A BEDROLL, VERSION 2

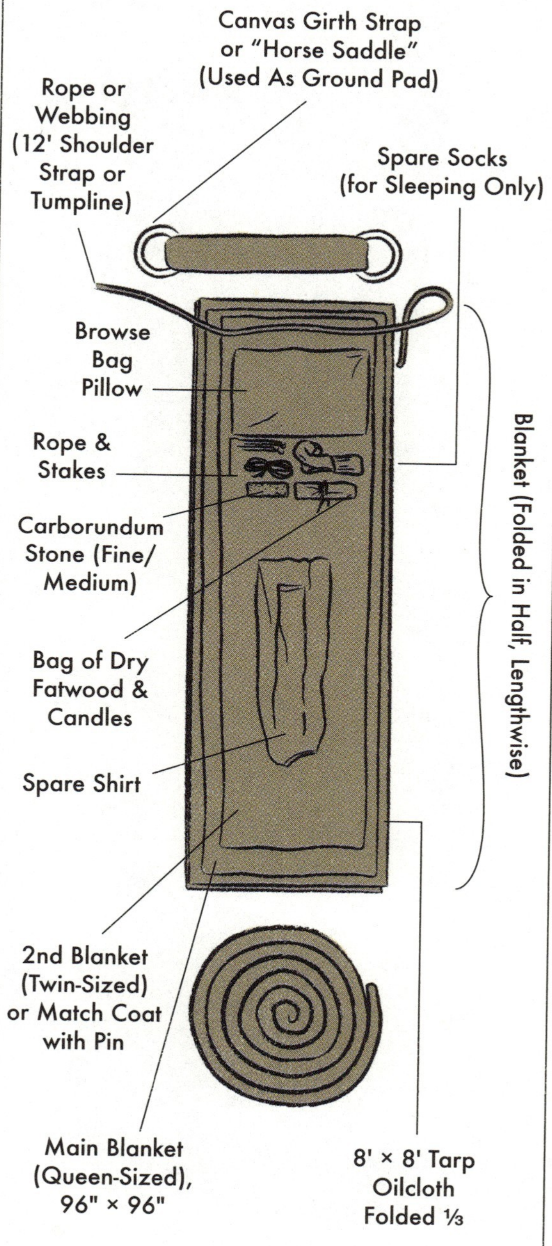

Rope or Webbing (12' Shoulder Strap or Tumpline)

Canvas Girth Strap or "Horse Saddle" (Used As Ground Pad)

Spare Socks (for Sleeping Only)

Browse Bag Pillow

Rope & Stakes

Carborundum Stone (Fine/Medium)

Bag of Dry Fatwood & Candles

Spare Shirt

Blanket (Folded in Half, Lengthwise)

2nd Blanket (Twin-Sized) or Match Coat with Pin

Main Blanket (Queen-Sized), 96" × 96"

8' × 8' Tarp Oilcloth Folded ⅓

Figure 5.21

As you saw in Chapter 1, you can also incorporate this bedroll as your backpack to carry all items needed and unroll everything once you arrive at camp. See **FIGURE 5.22** for an example of a bedroll pack.

BEDROLL PACK

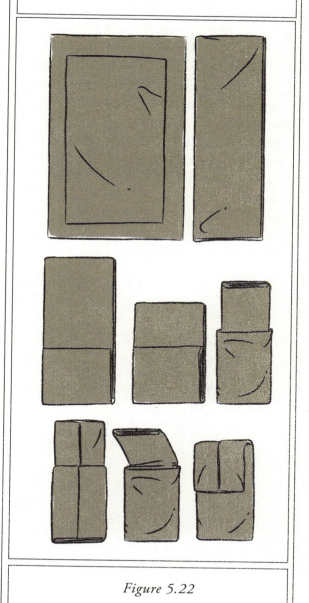

Figure 5.22

One of my favorite pieces of kit is the browse bed. This was written about by almost all of the old authors. In simple terms a browse bed is a sleeve (tube) of canvas material that can be used to construct a quick raised bed, either on logs or hung similar to a hammock. The one I carry is 12-ounce canvas and is about 7' long and 34" wide. The beauty of this system is that you can fill the tube with browse like leaves to make an insulative layer and still get off the ground as well. This system combined with the wool blankets and a tarp is tough to beat, and it does not have to be that heavy depending on choices of materials. This browse bed is also capable of being made into a satchel to hold the lot and attached to a pack frame like the Seneca or Roycraft. See **FIGURES 5.23 THROUGH 5.28** for examples.

SENECA FRAME, VERSION 2

Figure 5.24

ROYCRAFT TARP PACK

SENECA FRAME, VERSION 1

Figure 5.23

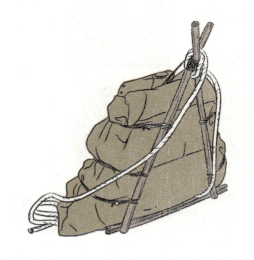

Figure 5.25

BROWSE BED, ANGLE 1

Figure 5.26

BROWSE BED, ANGLE 2

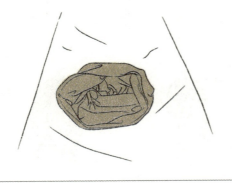

Figure 5.27

BROWSE BED, ANGLE 3

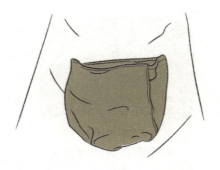

Figure 5.28

There is another setup known as the officer's bedroll that is basically a canvas outer shell with a large envelope for the blanket, smaller one for stuffing to make a pillow, and pockets for smaller gear choices and toiletries. See **FIGURES 5.29 THROUGH 5.32** for examples of these bedrolls.

OFFICER'S BEDROLL

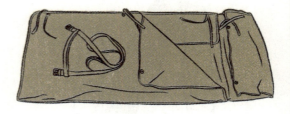

Figure 5.29

BEDROLL OVER PACK

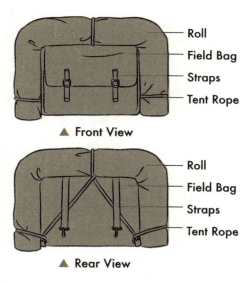

Roll
Field Bag
Straps
Tent Rope

▲ Front View

Roll
Field Bag
Straps
Tent Rope

▲ Rear View

Figure 5.30

CROSS-SLUNG BEDROLL

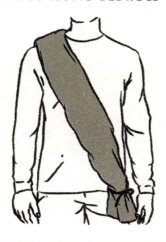

Figure 5.31

DIAGONAL WEAR BEDROLL

1.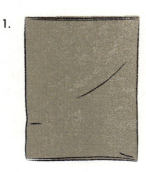

2.

3.    4.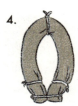

Figure 5.32

▲ Lay your bedroll materials flat on the ground. Roll the bottom sheet or tarp tightly. Tie both ends and in the middle. Next fold the roll in half where you tied it off in the middle. Tie those two ends together. Open the roll into a circle and wear it across your body (from shoulder to opposite hip).

CAMP FURNITURE

Part of bushcrafting is to bring in small pieces of gear, like a tarp, to get the camp started and then creating the rest from materials available in the forest. This would include many furnishings you may want around camp, from shelving to stools, chairs, and tables. Many can be made with the simple bushcraft trio of knife, saw, and axe, along the notches seen in "Creating Notches" in Chapter 2. See **FIGURES 5.33 THROUGH 5.44** for examples of furnishings you can make for your camp.

CHAIR

Figure 5.33

GEAR HANGERS

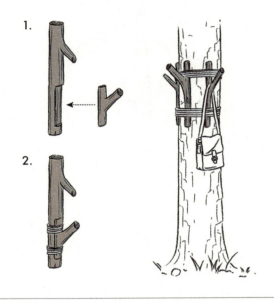

Figure 5.34

NET CHAIR

Figure 5.35

ROPE STOOL

Figure 5.36

ROPE LADDER

Figure 5.38

TROUGHS AND BOWLS

Figure 5.37

BUTTERFLY HAMMOCK CHAIR

Figure 5.39

CAMP TABLE

Figure 5.40

CAMP TOILET

Figure 5.41

BIRCH BARK CUP

1.
2.
3.
4.

Figure 5.42

WEAVE FOR MAKING ROLLAWAY OBJECTS

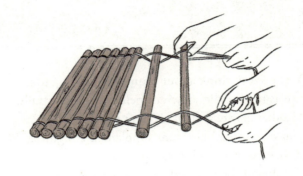

Figure 5.43

WOODLAND LOOM

Figure 5.44

CAMP LIGHTING

You need to think about sources of lighting to use as the fire dies down or before the fire is built. Headlamps are a main kit item obviously but you may sometimes want supplemental lighting devices around and in camp.

One of the best is the simple candle. Candles are very environmentally friendly and give off a warm natural glow that is very pleasant in camp. You can make your own by dipping wicking material into tallow.

In many countries oil lamps are still a go-to for woods lighting. A hurricane lantern gives off a nice warm lighting as well. A grease (fat) lamp can be manufactured by rending animal fat like deer tallow or raccoon lard and placing it in any natural container like clay or even a mussel shell with a wicking material like cattail fluff or corded mullein leaf. Any type of vegetable oils will also work with a wick and are also food safe for other uses. A slush lamp can be made out of basically any concave object that will hold animal fat or oil in a pool. You then add a natural wick material and can light that to create flame. These are usually very sooty, but effective for quick lighting. See **FIGURES 5.45 THROUGH 5.51** for a variety of lighting options you can either use or make in camp.

CANDLE HOLDERS

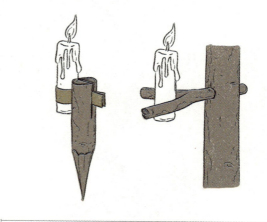

Figure 5.45

UCO CANDLE LANTERN

Figure 5.46

TALLOW CANDLES

Figure 5.47

DIETZ HURRICANE LANTERN

Figure 5.48

DIETZ OIL LAMP COOKER

Figure 5.49

GREASE LAMP

Figure 5.50

SLUSH LAMP

Figure 5.51

CHAPTER 6

FIRECRAFT

FIRE IS PROBABLY the single most important of skill sets next to knife craft. Your ability to make fire allows you to disinfect water, cook and preserve food, regulate your body temperature, fire-harden tools, signal for rescue in emergencies, and it gives your camp a homey ambiance unlike anything else. We have spent thousands of years telling stories and passing on ancestral knowledge around the campfire, and it will likely always be a large part of any overnight outdoor experience. Making a fire is not a difficult process. The difficulty comes as the materials become less ideal, and the ignition methods become more primitive in nature. In this chapter, you'll learn all you need to know about how to create fire in the wilderness.

ELEMENTS OF FIRE

The triangle of fire is heat, oxygen, and fuel. Without enough of any of these and without the proper balance of all three, fire will not be sustained. The balance can be the tricky part because so many variables affect it. Air current, humidity, direct moisture, quality of materials, ambient temperature, and weather can all affect what you must do to create a sustainable fire. See **FIGURE 6.1** for an illustration of the triangle of fire.

It is not difficult to start a fire with an open flame device, and many fires that burn thousands of acres are started by accident every year. But to do it on purpose how and when you want to or when you have to requires some skill and knowledge related to the necessary tools and materials.

TRIANGLE OF FIRE

Figure 6.1

TOOLS AND MATERIALS FOR FIRE

As we discussed in Chapter 2, you always want several ignition sources within your kit, including a good lighter, a large ferrocerium rod, and a nice magnifying glass. A good knife and maybe the saw from a Swiss Army knife will help with carving a bow drill kit, if desired. Having the tools to create fire and not relying on more primitive methods during an emergency is important, so even while practicing bushcraft you want to ensure that you have the means to make fire quickly when necessary.

When it comes to making fire, you should carry the proper modern equipment to make fire in emergencies: a lighter or storm matches, a good long ferrocerium rod, and a magnification lens are great options.

A storm match is a match that is created to burn in high wind or even if it gets wet. See **FIGURE 6.2** for an example of storm matches.

MAGNIFICATION LENS

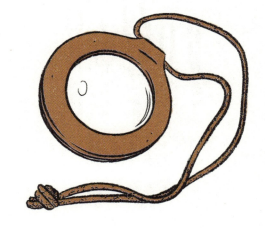

Figure 6.3

STORM MATCHES

Figure 6.2

See **FIGURES 6.3 AND 6.4** for examples of a magnification lens and how to use a magnification lens to ignite tinder material.

USING A MAGNIFICATION LENS TO LIGHT A FIRE

Figure 6.4

See **FIGURES 6.5–6.7** for examples of ferrocerium rods and how to use them.

VARIOUS FERROCERIUM RODS

Figure 6.5

STRIKING A FERROCERIUM ROD, VERSION 1

Figure 6.6

STRIKING A FERROCERIUM ROD, VERSION 2

Figure 6.7

While matches are a very traditional method of fire starting they are generally susceptible to wind unless they are storm matches. On the other hand, flint and steel is generally not so affected by wind and can be a very good option. When using flint and steel, you will need a high-carbon steel blade and a stone that is above 7 on the hardness scale. Quartz, chert, and flint will all work. The stone needs a sharp edge, so you may need to break it against another stone or with an axe handle to get the piece you need.

When we deal with flint and steel we are dealing with a much lower temperature spark than from a modern ferrocerium rod. Subsequently, the tinder source much be much more carefully selected as well. The spark is created by holding the stone still and striking a glancing blow to the stone with the high-carbon steel blade or vice versa. Both methods can be used. See **FIGURE 6.8** for an example of a flint-and-steel kit.

FLINT-AND-STEEL KIT

Figure 6.8

FIGURES 6.9 AND 6.10 show proper methods of striking flint and steel.

STRIKING FLINT AND STEEL, VERSION 1

Figure 6.9

STRIKING FLINT AND STEEL, VERSION 2

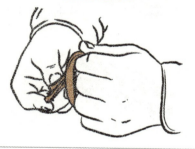

Figure 6.10

Making charred material is fairly easy using plants like cattail heads or even cotton or other natural materials from your kit. Seal it in a fireproof chamber like a bottle with the cup inverted over the lid or a tin that only lets gases escape through a small hole or loose seal but will not allow oxygen into the chamber when heated. Superheating the material will carbonize it, turning it to char.

The time this takes varies on the amount and type of material used, but never let oxygen into the chamber while the materials are still hot or they will burn up. Let the chamber cool and then look at the materials. If they are black and charred, they should work well. If they are brown you can put them in the fire longer.

See FIGURES 6.11 AND 6.12 for examples of creating charred material.

STRIKING A SPARK WITH A KNIFE

Figure 6.11

STRIKING A SPARK WITH A STEEL STRIKER

Figure 6.12

Tinder, kindling, and fuels are the main three components to making a sustainable fire, and the quality of these materials will have a large impact on success or failure. All three should be used in some form for every fire.

Tinder is highly combustible material that can take on many forms but should be the finest of materials that are contained in your initial fire lay. Sometimes in the case of receiving an ember from flint and steel, a magnification lens, or even a bow drill, this tinder may be held in the hand as to provide air flow from your mouth to accelerate the combustion process. It is then placed in the base of the fire lay to establish a sustainable fire.

Kindling is the next step in material size and should be very dry if possible and never larger than a pencil with pieces of pencil lead size being better. The biggest mistake I see from my students is the failure to have enough of this type and size material within their fire lay.

Fuel can be wood ranging in size from thumb-sized to logs, but again this must be in graduated form to create sustainability, with the initial lay having only the thumb-sized material with several pieces of fuel up to 2" in diameter at the ready. Once the fire is sustainable, larger fuel woods can be added. See **FIGURE 6.13** for the correct sequence of tinder, kindling, and fuel.

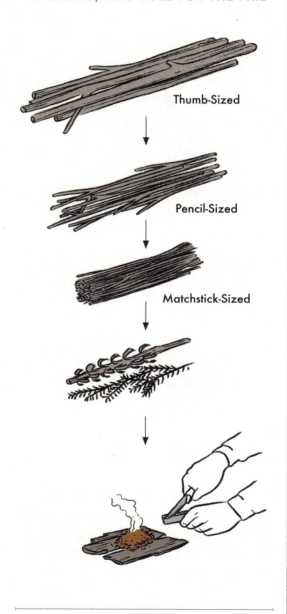

Thumb-Sized

Pencil-Sized

Matchstick-Sized

Figure 6.13

━ NEXT FIRE MENTALITY ━

Something that I call "next fire mentality" is, in many ways, where bushcraft meets survival. It's the understanding that you have gear to use if you have to use it but conserving that gear after its initial use is just as important. Fire is a perfect reflection of this mentality. If the first fire was started by a lighter, ferrocerium rod, or storm match, then subsequent fires should use fewer resources from your kit. This is the bushcraft mentality.

While in an emergency you should use the fastest method for making a fire, after that you should choose the one that best conserves your resources. That said, if you create a material from the landscape that will readily accept a smaller spark from the ferrocerium rod or will ignite readily with the use of a magnification lens then you are taking advantage of nature's storehouse and practicing a bushcraft mentality. Charring material is the best way to make this possible. Many plant piths, punky woods, and some fungus will char and this can be used for creating the ember for combustion of the next fire. In my mind this is where a magnification lens and the high-carbon steel knife (flint and steel) really shine, as both are virtually limitless in use and conserve your more precious resource for times when these may not work or when your skill level does not permit you to overcome some variable like weather to accomplish another fire.

Open flame devices like lighters and matches are great for emergency fire making and should never be left out of your kit. If you have processed material correctly and you have a sheltered or windless area to start with, you should have no trouble establishing a sustainable fire.

Bushcraft Tip

Many trees have natural oils and resins that act as accelerants. These can be very useful, as barks and wood will have a much longer burn time than plant fibers. The two most significant sources for your purpose are birch barks and pine resins. Both of these require different types of processing. Birch bark can be peeled from the tree, but its intended use will decide the type of processing. Remember that any time you are attempting ignition by sparks from a rod, you will need lots of surface area to catch the sparks. The same holds true with barks such as birch; you'll need to shred it as finely as possible to expose many surfaces that can be ignited by sparks. If you have an open flame, the bark will readily burn straight off the tree.

The so-called "bird's nest" (not a real nest, but one you'll make) is what you'll use for initial combustion when making fires by ember. You'll place the ember into a bird's nest and then coax it to flame by blowing into the nest to increase the heat rising through the materials. The key to the bird's nest lies in the processing and stacking of the materials. You will need coarse, medium, and fine tinders intermixed and made into something that resembles a bird's nest, with some of the finest materials in the center where the ember is to be placed. See **FIGURE 6.14** for an example of the bird's nest and **FIGURE 6.15** for an example of air flow through the bird's nest.

Bushcraft Tip

Poplars are some of the best trees for construction and combustion. They make excellent fire sets for primitive combustion (bow drill) and have an inner bark that when dry can be processed into highly flammable bird's nests and tinder bundles.

BIRD'S NEST

Figure 6.14

AIR FLOW THROUGH THE BIRD'S NEST

Figure 6.15

TINDER BUNDLES

A tinder bundle is a stack of materials slightly more course than what you'd use to create a bird's nest. The difference is that a bird's nest accepts an ember and a tinder bundle is usually used with high-temperature sparks from a ferrocerium rod or open flame. With open flame, you can be less particular with material processing (the breaking down of materials to expose surface area and make them finer) and coarser materials can be used. If the material cannot be broken down to hair-like fibers, or the material has dampness to it, or if the material feels cold on the cheek, then open flame in a tinder bundle is a better ignition source than non-open flame methods. Like all tinder materials, the more you have, the better the longevity of heat to ignite progressively larger materials. Things like grasses burn faster than dried inner barks from trees. See **FIGURE 6.16** for an example of a tinder bundle.

TINDER BUNDLE

Figure 6.16

TWIG BUNDLES

A twig bundle, a small bundle of sticks or dry weed stems that are very dry and about ⅛" in diameter, is best used for open-flame ignition when better tinder materials may not be available. You want the twig bundle materials to be as dry as possible since you are really forgoing the true tinder portion (the use of the finer materials like inner barks used in a tinder bundle or a bird's nest) of the ignition process. The best materials for this bundle will be dead weed stems or the smallest of dry twigs. Something with a natural oil like dry dead pine twigs will help as well. Leave plenty of air space within the twig bundle and hold the flame about ⅓" below the base, keeping the bundle at an angle to allow the heat and flame to rise up the material. See **FIGURE 6.17** for an example of a twig bundle.

TWIG BUNDLE

Figure 6.17

Making feather sticks has long been a way to create fine tinder materials from larger pieces of wood. Feather sticks are sticks whose tops have been altered to include shavings that are so fine they curl over. Many older illustrations have them looking fairly small. Some more modern books make them look like many finely shaven veneers, stacked at the end of a stick. In my experience, for the intended purpose of the feather stick, something between the two is adequate. If you always begin the fine shaving on a corner of the wood and then rotate the piece with each slice, you will have a fairly easy time of it. When trying to make shavings, take advantage of the slicing motion of the blade using its length at a slight angle to perpendicular and then adjust the blade angle to the work for the desired thickness. See **FIGURE 6.18** for an example of what a feather stick looks like. See **FIGURE 6.19** for an example of how to make a feather stick.

Bushcraft Tip

The general rule of thumb is that you should never need more than five seconds of flame from a lighter to obtain ignition. Feather sticks will help with this.

FEATHER STICK

Figure 6.18

MAKING A FEATHER STICK

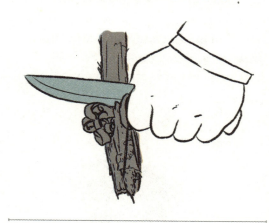

Figure 6.19

Some plants have parts that can be used as a tinder source. Many are what we call flash tinders. In other words they are highly combustible, but they burn very quickly so other tinders should be used with them to help sustain the flame to ignite kindling. Queen of the meadow, the fluff or down from the cattail head, and thistle down are good examples.

Another natural material that will take a low-temperature spark from the flint-and-steel method is the ovum of the milkweed pod. This is the center of the pod where the seeds were attached before dispersion. It will usually be left in the pod and you can just harvest and use or save for later. It is best to tear the ovum in half and expose some fibers to have next to the striker for sparks to easily ignite. See Chapter 10 for an example of milkweed ovum.

Birch and pine are highly flammable. They can be used even when damp or in wet weather. With birch, the tree has betula oil within the bark, so open flame will ignite the bark with very little processing save making some small strips. With pine we are looking for the fat- or resin-laden areas of the tree. This takes place as the sap rises and settles but generally can be found anywhere a branch connects to the tree itself or on a standing dead tree near the base of the trunk and within the roots. Once a resin-laden piece of pine is found it can be processed in several ways, depending on the ignition source. If you have

open flame for ignition then small splits will burn like matches. If you have only a hot spark of a ferrocerium rod, you can create fine scrapings with the back of your knife and then ignite. This source is not a good source for the weaker spark of flint and steel or for a magnification lens.

There are also many types of fungus used around the world as tinder sources. True tinder fungus *Inonotus obliquus* (chaga) grows mostly on birch trees and in cooler northern areas of the Eastern Woodlands. There are other funguses sometime called tinder fungus like *Fomes fomentarius*. These are a false tinder fungus and do not act the same with low spark ignition as the aforementioned chaga. With any of these materials you are looking for the soft inner parts of the fungus under the hard outer shell (the amadou).

The amadou of hoof fungus that grows on birch, maple, and beech is generally gray to off-white in color. The amadou layer is just below the outer hard shell. This soft layer can be scraped with a saw or knife to harvest, or it can be carefully peeled away. See **FIGURES 6.20 THROUGH 6.23** for an example of scraping amadou from hoof fungus.

HOOF FUNGUS

Figure 6.20

SCRAPING AMADOU

Figure 6.22

AMADOU LAYER

Amadou Layer

Figure 6.21

AMADOU SHAVINGS

Figure 6.23

Many of these funguses have a fairly thick layer of material called the trauma layer that when processed and dried looks a bit like brain-tanned leather. This process is a bit dogged and requires the careful removal of the outer hard bark-type material as well as the sporing tubes from the bottom. Then the amadou is boiled to open the fibers and remove glucose. Once this material is boiled for a few hours, the material is pounded to further loosen the fibers and dried to get the tan-like substance that will take a low-temperature spark.

One of the more common types of fungus in the Eastern Woodlands is the bracket fungus. This fungus grows on living trees or dead wood, forming one or more shelf-like projections that are the spore-producing bodies. The cracked cap polypore is an example of this type of fungus. This fungus is not as easily used for flint-and-steel ignition although I have gotten it to work with a high-temperature spark or by solar ignition. The best way I have found to use this is to remove it from the tree, take a saw and cut into the softer underside, creating a dust. This dust can then be spread out in a thin layer to attempt a flint-and-steel ignition or scraped into a small pile for other types of ignition. It will then form a coagulated coal that can be transferred to a bird's nest. See **FIGURES 6.24 AND 6.25** for examples of bracket fungus and cracked cap polypore.

BRACKET FUNGUS

Figure 6.24

CRACKED CAP POLYPORE

Figure 6.25

— FRICTION FIRE —

When it comes to friction fire in the Eastern Woodlands the bow drill is the best option. The mechanical advantage gained from this simple machine will overcome many issues with material caused by high humidity and damp weather.

To make a friction fire, you first have to consider material selection as this is the most important step in the process. Woods that are too hard may work if you have perfect form and plenty of energy, but softer woods will work much better and faster. Some woods to consider are cedar, both red and white; any poplar species, including cottonwood; tulip poplar, which is actually in the magnolia family; willow; and pine. These are softer-wood trees (don't confuse conifer and deciduous as soft and hard woods for this discussion).

You will need four main components—the hearth board, the spindle, the bow, and the bearing block—for making the bow drill. Many times three of the components can come from the same tree; we will discuss this as we go.

The hearth board is the flat piece of wood that is on the bottom with a notch cut into it for creating the coal or ember. The spindle is the round piece that is part of the drill that will also help create the ember. The bow is what will rotate the spindle on the board and regulates the speed the spindle turns by manual force. The bearing block is the top portion of the machine that holds the spindle on the upper side and allows rotation using the bow. You are creating a simple machine like any drill that reciprocates on an axis created between the hearth board and the hand-hold driven by a bow and your own energy. See FIGURE 6.26 for an example of a bow drill set.

BOW DRILL SET

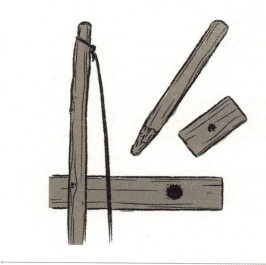

Figure 6.26

FIGURE 6.27 shows how the parts are assembled.

ASSEMBLED BOW DRILL SET

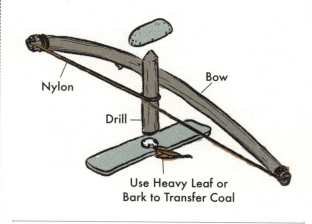

Nylon

Bow

Drill

Use Heavy Leaf or Bark to Transfer Coal

Figure 6.27

It is best if the handhold or bearing block is green wood, although many other options can also be used. See **FIGURE 6.28** for some examples of bearing blocks.

VARIOUS BEARING BLOCKS

Figure 6.28

Pictured are three options. The first one is a commercial handhold made to be used as a flint-and-steel striker and ferrocerium rod striker as well; the second is a hardwood bearing block; and the third is made from a section of deer antler. Any of these will work as well as things like a natural stone that has been pecked to form a divot or found to naturally have one.

The bow should be of green wood but shouldn't be really flexible. It should be about the length of your arm from pit to cupped hand. This will give the best mechanical advantage by increasing rotations of the spindle with each stroke. The two things to avoid here are a heavy bow or a short bow as these will limit you both in rotations for energy spent as well as energy to move and hold level a heavier bow. I like to use a branch with a fork in one end as my bow since this alleviates the need for notches to attach a string. A simple saw kerf that the cord can be wrapped into on the other end and finished with a clove hitch will work nicely. Do not make the cordage overtight

on the bow as this will make loading the spindle difficult.

I generally find it best if the hearth and spindle are of the same material because this saves you from having to look for two different types of material and because these can often be taken from the same piece of wood, which results in a lower gathering time. I suggest if possible taking a portion of a dead but not rotting tree about 4" in diameter and 12" long to produce the set. This will give a nice board from the center and if split three times at least four options for this portion and two for the hearth. See **FIGURE 6.29** for an example of how to cut.

HOW TO CUT A SPINDLE AND HEARTH

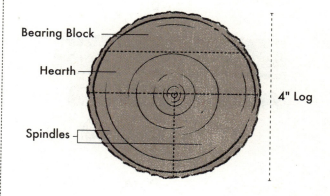

Figure 6.29

Starting with the center cut, this will be where the hearth comes from. It should be the driest area of the piece, and it should give you the largest area of sap or white wood available from the log itself. You want to avoid any areas of heavy resins or heartwood if possible. Split this again down the pith center to give you two boards and select the best one, free of knots or twisted grain pattern. Note you will want this board to be about 1" thick when split out, so bear this in mind when making your log splits.

Once you have figured out which side you will use for the hearth board, you can begin to square up the piece. It is important that the board not rock around and that it is level on the ground when making an ember. Movement will cause a loss in form; good form is important for making the process smooth. Now you'll need to set the hearth board aside to make the spindle. You need to know the diameter of your spindle before making your hearth board, so this is the reason for the break. From one of the other pieces you should be able to split again and have plenty of material to make a spindle the right length and diameter. **FIGURE 6.30** shows an example of a spindle made this way.

SPINDLE

Figure 6.30

You want the spindle to be about the length of the distance between the pinky finger and the thumb of an outstretched hand or about 9". Make it a bit long in the rough stages. When you're done carving the spindle, you want it to end up about ¾" to 1" in diameter and to be straight and round as possible. Once this step is complete, you can refine the shape, tapering one end to somewhat of a point, and rounding the opposite or working end by chamfering the edges to a dome shape but leaving the facets in place.

FIGURE 6.31 shows the bearing block end of the spindle.

BEARING BLOCK END OF THE SPINDLE

Figure 6.31

Now that you have your spindle, you can get back to the hearth board. First you will need to create a divot or a place for the spindle to sit and initially begin to spin for burning-in the hearth board. Use the point of your knife to cut this divot shallow on the top of the hearth. To figure out where you want this divot in relation to the board use the diameter of your finished spindle and half again as a measurement, and then start about 2" from the end of the board. See **FIGURE 6.32** for an example of a spindle and a hearth board with a divot.

HEARTH WITH DIVOT AND SPINDLE

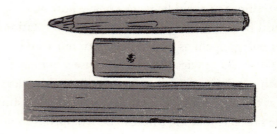

Figure 6.32

Now make a bearing block, which will be placed at the top of the spindle to hold downward pressure on the spindle against the fire board. This piece is the one that will give you the most headache during operation of the set. It seems a simple thing but it is critical to the smooth operation of the entire set. To make a natural wood handhold, find a tree that is green or a branch about 3" in diameter and cut a section the width of your fist. Split this in half on just one side of the heartwood and make a small divot in the center of the heartwood side a bit smaller than the hearth divot as the spindle is smaller at the top.

Now comes the process of testing the machine and making sure it is capable of creating an ember. You want to do this prior to cutting a notch so that you get a good notch orientation to the spindle divot, and it will allow you to look at color and smoke created before adding more work to the hearth board.

Set up in the same manner you would to make a complete ember but only rotate the spindle at medium speed and until the board becomes blackened in the divot and smoke begins to appear. See **FIGURES 6.33 AND 6.34** on how to load the spindle.

LOAD THE SPINDLE, STEP 1

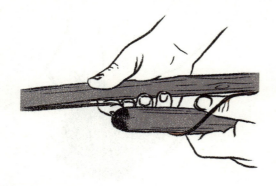

Figure 6.33

LOAD THE SPINDLE, STEP 2

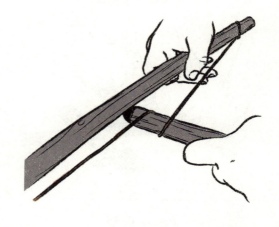

Figure 6.34

Now comes the time to make our notch and finish up the set before making our coal. We will want the notch oriented so that it is approximately three-fourths the width of the burned divot, and apexes at the burn-in itself but no deeper. This can be accomplished by saw or axe.

Now you can begin the task of creating an ember from this simple machine using the same position that you used for burn-in. One thing to remember here is that we want friction first and speed second. We are creating an ember that is much like fire or charred cloth in many ways: the oxygen flow comes from the open notch, the fuel is what we create by grinding down the board and spindle through rotations, and the heat will be accomplished by speed and friction together, so we must first have fuel before ignition. A medium speed of operation on the bow and solid downward pressure will accomplish this. See **FIGURE 6.35** for the correct position to run the bow drill.

CORRECT POSITION FOR RUNNING THE BOW DRILL

Figure 6.35

As you are drilling pay attention to the materials you are creating in the notch and how much there is. Black material is already burnt most of the time so you want it dark brown. Too much pressure can burn it and too much speed can do the same, so it is a happy medium at first. **FIGURE 6.36** shows how to fill the notch with material.

FILLING THE NOTCH WITH MATERIAL

Figure 6.36

Once the notch is filled by material you can increase speed to add heat, and this will ignite the ember from the top. Smoke should be rolling from the set most of the time after the first five to ten strokes of the bow. Once you have a good pile of fuel material, another ten to twenty strokes at higher speed will generally be enough. When you think you have a live ember you need to stop slowly and carefully so as not to disturb the ember at first. Set your things aside, gently lift the board, and tap the ember free on a welcome mat—a sliver of bark or something to use for transfer and to keep the ember off the ground—that you placed under the board before starting. Wait until it has actually turned red on the top and you see the actual ember before transferring carefully to the bird's nest. Once in the nest let the coal settle a moment and lift the nest, folding it in slightly (not tightly) to protect the ember. Begin to slowly blow air on the coal while the nest is slightly elevated to allow heat to rise through the nest. As the ember gets larger you can blow a bit harder until you have flame. At that point invert the nest to allow flame to again rise into the bundle and place in the fire lay. **FIGURE 6.37** shows how to place the ember in the bird's nest.

PLACING THE EMBER IN THE BIRD'S NEST

Figure 6.37

CHAPTER 7

NAVIGATION

WHEN IT COMES to bushcraft I believe navigation is one of the most under-studied and under-utilized of all skills. If you are trying to connect with the natural world, you need to try to use the tools it provides for you in navigation as well. In this chapter you'll learn how to use the natural world to find your way.

— PRIMITIVE NAVIGATION —

There are many different forms of natural navigation tools as well as many ways to utilize them. One of the things you need to understand is that, while the primitive navigation tools found in this section many never be as accurate for use on the fly as a magnetic compass, they're still very useful. With some simple understanding they can be very accurate for moving in a chosen direction and many are very repeatable over distance as well.

One thing that's important to keep in mind is that the sun rises in the east, sets in the west, and travels in a southern arc across the sky. So it is easy enough to understand cardinal directions in the morning and evening and we will be fairly accurate, again on the fly. Anytime you are facing the sun during the day you are facing a southern direction and the closer to noon the closer to south. But just as you do not want to rely on a compass for this you also do not want to rely on a watch. In this section, you'll learn how to figure out time and direction without modern pieces in the field.

Bushcraft Tip

Remember that the moon travels in roughly the same arc as the sun, and at night makes a great navigational aid. It rises in the east and sets in the west, with its zenith hours of 10 p.m.–2 a.m. being in a southerly direction when you are looking at the moon.

Plants tend to always grow toward the most light due to auxin. Auxin is a plant hormone that causes elongation of the plant cells to help them grow toward sunlight. For example, many times trees will have the heaviest foliage and branches on the southeastern side of the tree. Most plants will tend to lean toward the southeast in the northern hemisphere; however, there are exceptions like in clearings and one should always use multiple sources when using primitive methods to verify findings. See **FIGURE 7.1** for an example of how plants bend toward the sun.

Prevailing winds can force plants and trees to bend over time but may also show direction by making the prevailing wind side of a tree wet in a driving rain while the opposite side is dry. Growth rings can also help tell the side of the tree that has gotten the most sunlight, which reveals a southern direction as well. **FIGURE 7.2** shows an example of how a misshapen tree trunk can indicate direction.

HOW PLANTS BEND TOWARD SUNLIGHT

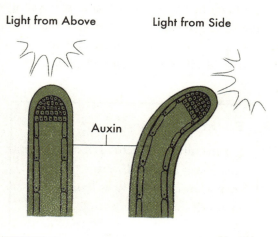

Figure 7.1

GROWTH RINGS OF A TREE INDICATING DIRECTION

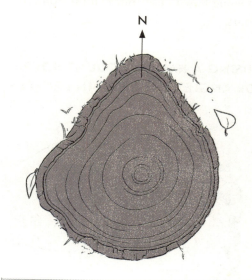

Figure 7.2

Time is relative when you're in nature and is different than the time of day in your modern life. You must forget what time it may or may not be and think more in hours of daylight and degrees of sun angle to the horizon to get better at navigation using the sun. To see how many hours the sun has been above the horizon or how many hours are left of daylight you can count hands from the horizon to the base of the sun or vice versa. Each hour will represent approximately 15 degrees of sun angle as well. See **FIGURE 7.3** for a chart showing how to use your hand to count hours.

USING A HAND TO COUNT HOURS OR ANGLE OF THE SUN IN DEGREES

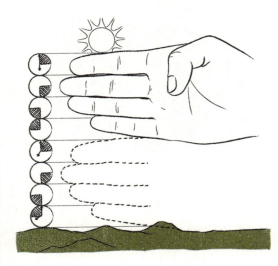

Figure 7.3

You should understand that based on the twenty-four-hour day, the earth's rotation makes the sun appear to move approximately 15 degrees every hour. Looking at the sky as half a clock face, this gives us the 180-degree semicircle broken down into twelve segments, with each segment encompassing 15 degrees. You'll use this to track the twelve hours of daytime and the twelve hours we consider nighttime.

For the purposes of natural navigation you need to assume that the majority of the year there will be about 180 degrees of travel from sunup to sundown or east-to-west travel. This will be less accurate on longer and shorter days of the year. However, it will be close enough for general use. If you use the same methods throughout a trip, you will at least travel in the same general direction even if that is a few degrees off true or magnetic north, as you are dealing with solar navigation.

Bushcraft Tip
When using any method of navigation to get general direction other than a compass, check at least three methods for verification.

144   BUSHCRAFT ILLUSTRATED

Earlier, in **FIGURE 7.3**, I showed you how to use your hand to determine time by measuring the sun's distance from the horizon. You can also use your hand to determine the angle of the sun, which can then be translated to hours as well. In the same method used to figure hours with the understanding that the earth moves approximately 15 degrees per hour (depending on time of year this may vary), you can factor three hours or hands as 45 degrees. So, if the sun is at a 45-degree angle in the sky in the morning, it is about three hours after sunrise. See **FIGURE 7.4** for how to calculate the angle of the sun with your hand.

USING YOUR HAND TO CALCULATE ANGLES

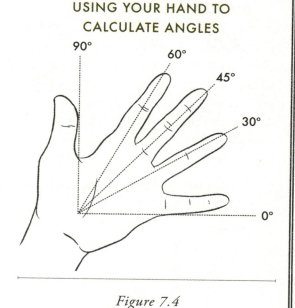

Figure 7.4

FINDING CARDINAL DIRECTIONS

Once you understand how to count the hours the sun has been up or the hours left until it sets, you have lots of possibilities for navigation instruments on the fly. Determining a simple cardinal direction of northerly should be no more difficult than using your own shadow on the ground in relation to the sun's angle deduced by hours above horizon (morning hours) to adjust yourself back to a northerly direction. See **FIGURE 7.5** for an illustration of this method.

HORIZON LINE ADJUSTMENT METHOD

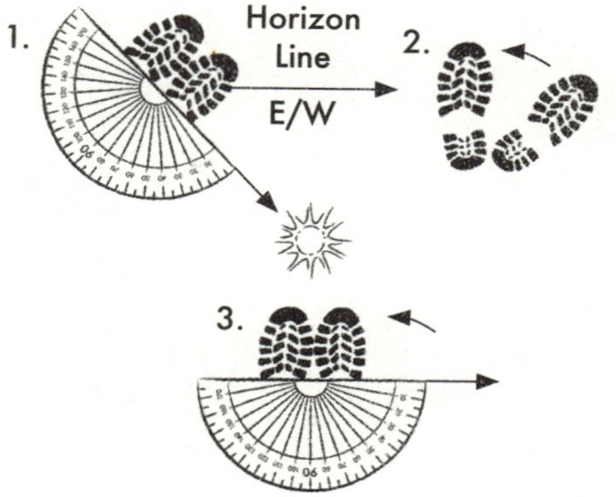

Figure 7.5

CHAPTER 7. NAVIGATION

SHADOW STICK METHOD

There are many standard ways as well to find a simple cardinal direction. For example, you can calculate direction by noticing where a shadow falls from a stick you place and tracking the shadow's movement over a period of time. See **FIGURE 7.6** for an example of how to do this.

SHADOW STICK METHOD

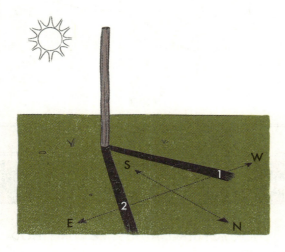

Figure 7.6

OTTOMANI SUN COMPASS

Another method you can try, once the shadow stick has been set, is to build the Ottomani sun compass. Use the shadow stick for calibration. This will need to be done at least a couple of times during each month if used longer term, but it gives a portable instrument to determine direction of travel on a sunny day. This device is a bit less accurate than shadow boards based on a curved line (you'll learn more about them later on in this chapter) but nonetheless it is very useful short term. And if it is used time and again on the same trip it will give repeatable results.

To make this device a small slab of wood is suspended by three strings or pieces of natural cordage (if you can find some that's smooth) for leveling, and a gnomon or pointer, which will be used to cast a shadow from the sun on the board, is placed on the board's bottom-side length. The gnomon needs to be small enough to cast a shadow partway across the board. Make this board a small rectangle and attempt to have true 90-degree angles between the board and the gnomon, as best you can. Placing a gnomon on the southern edge of a pointed stick will work for this. Then, once the board is laid on the ground parallel to the east-west line of the shadow stick, draw a line across the length of the board where the shadow is cast.

If the device is then picked up it will face north if the shadow is touching the line when the device is suspended and level during travel or when you stop to find a bearing. See **FIGURE 7.7** for an example of how to make this device.

CALIBRATED OTTOMANI SUN COMPASS

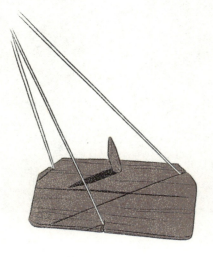

Figure 7.7

HORIZON BOARDS

You can use the circle like a clock or a 360-degree protractor in several ways as well to make an expedient navigational device for not only quickly determining a cardinal direction but also short distance navigation allowing a leap frog from one object to another to travel a relatively straight line and somewhat eliminate lateral drift. (Leap frogging means traveling only a short distance to a near object within a bearing line that you will not lose sight of during travel.)

Once you have anything large enough to draw a circle on—this could be paper or wood, a notebook, whatever you have—as well as something to write with (and this could be charcoal), you can make a circle about 4"–6" and bisect it like a simple pie. This gives you four 90-degree angles that are split at 45 degrees per line, or three hours of sun travel between each line. You can do one of two things with this. If you want a quick reference to find north, you can place a stick into the ground that will cast a shadow completely across the board. With the center line as the horizon and the top being noon, you can deduce at least northerly/southerly directions by facing the sun. You then see how many hours the sun is above the horizon and adjust the board to make the shadow cast across the appropriate degree line on the board and the top will be northerly. See **FIGURE 7.8** for an example of a horizon board.

HORIZON BOARD

Figure 7.8

SHADOW BOARDS

Once you understand the simple method used to make a horizon board you can put a gnomon in the center of the board and use this for the same purpose, but you can also carry it to use to maintain your direction. Use the hours-and-hands method to determine orientation of the board (assuming this is on a board, or something you can maintain level or lay on flat ground). Understanding that the shadow will only move 15 degrees or so every hour will allow you to pick a distant object you will not lose sight of in a particular travel direction. Upon arrival at that waypoint, you can set the board down again and reset for the same travel direction, stopping every so often to recheck the sun as it will move and you will need to adjust for that on the shadow board to maintain the same direction of travel.

See **FIGURE 7.9** for an example of a simple shadow board compass and **FIGURE 7.10** for a shadow board using a notebook. Again, none of these methods are exact, but they are much better than having nothing and will help eliminate lateral drift.

SHADOW BOARD COMPASS

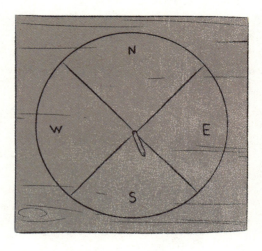

Figure 7.9

SHADOW BOARD ON A NOTEBOOK

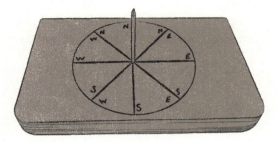

Figure 7.10

A more complex method of using a shadow board is to track the sun for an entire day, marking the shadow tips about every 15 degrees, giving a curved line, as opposed to the Ottomani straight inferred line. This will function the same way suspended to level and will give an accurate reading of north over distance throughout the day. It too must be recalibrated about every two weeks. Keep in mind that the Ottomani line is straight, but as the sun actually casts an arced shadow line there is some loss in accuracy.

See **FIGURES 7.11 AND 7.12** for examples of the Ottomani line differential.

OTTOMANI LINE DIFFERENTIAL COMPARED TO THE SUN'S TRUE ARC

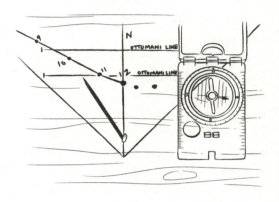

Figure 7.11

ANOTHER OTTOMANI LINE DIFFERENTIAL

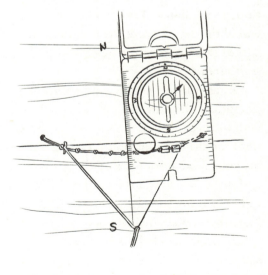

Figure 7.12

TRAVELING SHADOW COMPASS METHOD (PATHFINDER SUN COMPASS)

For a traveling shadow compass, you will select a smaller piece of wood, at least 5" × 7", that will act as a miniature traveling shadow stick. Place this board lengthwise to the east-west line you have made by the shadow stick method. Drill a hole into the center of the board, and place a small stick in the hole. This stick will cast a shadow on the board. Track the movement of the sun about every hour. As a reference, the sun moves about 15 degrees per hour. This time, mark the end of the shadow right on the board. You can use a round pot or something similar to make the mark almost like you would with a protractor. Mark everything right on the board. Place a dot on the board every hour through a full day of sun, and then, at the end of the day, connect the dots to form a curved scale. Now you have created your own sundial.

Whenever you need to find a direction or estimate the time, simply hold the board with the back toward the sun and rotate it until the shadow touches the curved line. Set your sundial compass on the ground and this will give you the cardinal directions again from your standing position. Note that this sundial will only be accurate for about 30 days before the shadow length starts to change along with the seasons.

See **FIGURE 7.13** for an example of a sun compass. **FIGURES 7.14, 7.15, AND 7.16** are examples of how you can segment a full circle to determine degrees or hours of the day.

SUN COMPASS

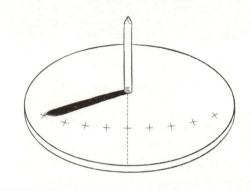

Figure 7.13

DIVIDING A CIRCLE INTO HOURS

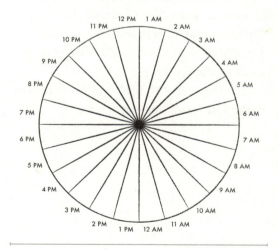

Figure 7.14

ROSE COMPASS—CIRCLE DIVIDED INTO DEGREES AND CARDINAL DIRECTIONS

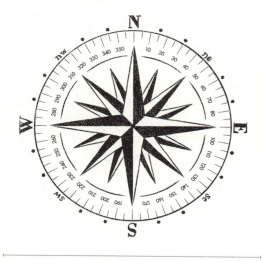

Figure 7.15

DIVIDING A CIRCLE INTO ANGLES

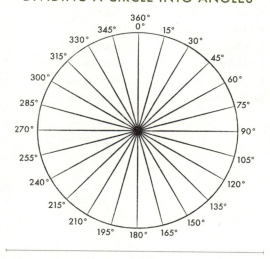

Figure 7.16

LUNAR AND CELESTIAL NAVIGATION

Let's talk about lunar and celestial navigation as well for a couple of quick methods. The North Star is a good reliable sign of north for the northern hemisphere and the Southern Cross for the southern hemisphere. See **FIGURE 7.17** for an example of how to locate the North Star.

LOCATING THE NORTH STAR

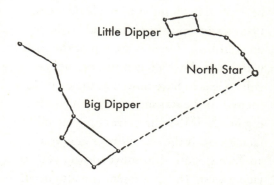

Figure 7.17

Another simple method for quick reference is the moon. On a crescent moon, a line drawn from tip to tip and then down to the horizon will indicate south.

One of the best methods to find a general direction at night is LURD (left, up, right, down). This method does not require the moon or any certain star to be visible. It should be used with a star in mid-sky that will not disappear from cloud cover for at least twenty minutes and should be verified by doing it a couple of times. Plant a stick in the ground and lie down on your back. Line up the top of the stick with a star. After a few minutes, the star will appear to have moved as the earth has rotated. If the star moves left, you are facing north. If the star moves up, you are facing east. If the star moves right, you are facing south. If it moves down, you are facing west. The movement can also occur in combination: right and down would be southwest. This method will work for any star except the North Star (**FIGURE 7.17** shows how to locate the North Star). See **FIGURE 7.18** for a diagram of the LURD method.

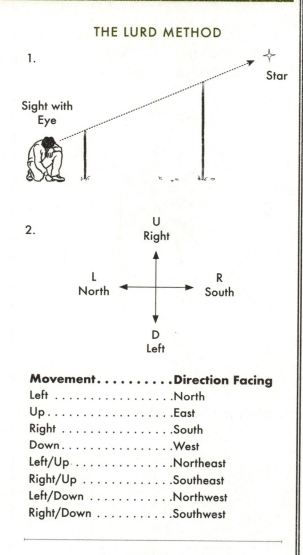

THE LURD METHOD

1. Sight with Eye — Star

2.

| U Right |
| L North — R South |
| D Left |

Movement	Direction Facing
Left	North
Up	East
Right	South
Down	West
Left/Up	Northeast
Right/Up	Southeast
Left/Down	Northwest
Right/Down	Southwest

Figure 7.18

— COMPASSES AND MAPS —

You don't always want to rely on natural methods of determining direction and location. For making long treks, you'll probably prefer to use a map and magnetic compass. The main reason for any navigation method whether improvised or a true compass is to allow you to walk a straight line over distance. Even if you are using a primitive method you should still be able to walk a straight line and avoid lateral drift.

COMPASSES

The reason compass use is so important is that without one, you'll have a hard time walking in a straight line, particularly over long distances. Lateral drift, which affects everyone, causes you to move slightly left or right as you walk. This is a problem if you can't see the object you're aiming for (perhaps because of an obstruction or because it's a long way off).

Bushcraft Tip

Not all compasses are created equal, and there are many types on the market today. Whatever compass you choose to use should act as a navigational device, signaling device for emergencies, mirror used for first aid as well as daily hygiene, and a tool capable of fire-starting by solar ignition.

BASIC COMPASS USE

A compass is used to establish a bearing, usually described as your position of travel in relationship to magnetic north. If you consider magnetic north to be zero, then a bearing of 15 degrees is slightly to the northeast. Most compasses have a needle that is two different colors, usually red/white or orange/white. The white side of the needle points south, and the colored area points north. The "front" or "top" of the compass is where the mirror is, so if you open the compass and look into the mirror, your compass is pointed to the front. Under the bezel ring of the compass should be an outlined arrow or set of lines that move as the bezel ring is moved. See **FIGURE 7.19** for an example of a survival compass.

SURVIVAL COMPASS

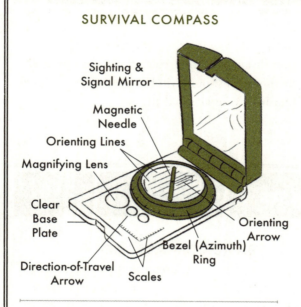

Sighting & Signal Mirror

Magnetic Needle

Orienting Lines

Magnifying Lens

Clear Base Plate

Direction-of-Travel Arrow

Scales

Bezel (Azimuth) Ring

Orienting Arrow

Figure 7.19

Aim the sighting device on your compass lid at a distant object in the direction you are headed. Hold the compass centered on your body with your arms slightly away from your body. Tilt the mirror enough that you can see both the object in the distance through the "V" and the bezel ring on your compass. The needle on your compass will always point north, so at this point move your bezel ring so that the outline, or "doghouse," lines up in such a way that the north needle is inside. You will then have the bearing at the top of your compass. At this point, if you lower your compass and keep the north needle within the line in the bezel ring as you walk, you will be walking a straight line or exact bearing.

FIGURE 7.20 shows how to use the compass to get your bearing.

SIGHTING WITH THE COMPASS TO GET YOUR BEARING

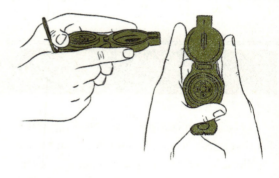

Figure 7.20

Bushcraft Tip

Sooner or later when traveling by compass, you will stray off course. When this happens, you should attempt a reverse azimuth to return to the last known point. A reverse azimuth just means traveling 180 degrees in the opposite direction from where you were going. The easiest method is to simply look at your compass as if it were a clock. If your current bearing is at 12 o'clock, rotate the bezel to the 6 o'clock number, and you have the reverse azimuth.

TERRAIN FEATURES AND MAPS

Remember that a topographic map is a two-dimensional image of a three-dimensional surface. So if you understand what you are looking at on the map, you can visualize what it looks like in real life. There are five colors on most topographical maps:

1. **Brown** is used for contour lines—lines that show elevation.
2. **Green** is used for vegetation—the darker the green, the more dense the vegetation.
3. **Blue** is used for water sources—creeks, streams, rivers, lakes, ponds.
4. **Black** is generally a man-made object—a trail, a railway, or a building.
5. **Red** shows major roadways such as highways.

And there are five terrain features you'll want to watch out for:

1. **Hilltops** are the highest point of elevation in a rise, offering opportunities for overlook.
2. A **ridgeline** is a series of hilltops, enabling high ground travel.
3. A **saddle** is a low area between two hilltops, offering windbreak for camps without sacrificing elevation.
4. A **draw** is the reduction in elevation from a saddle with high ground on both sides. This is usually a good runoff point for water and in many cases leads to a valley.

5. A **valley** is a low elevation running between ridgelines. These areas hold runoff and are the best places to look for unmarked streams. If they hold water, the higher ground above them will be excellent for ambushing game that goes to the water to drink. Most valleys are also good trapping locations.

See **FIGURE 7.21** for an example of a topographical map.

TOPOGRAPHICAL MAP

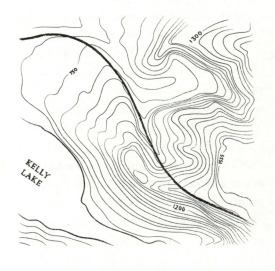

Figure 7.21

USING THE MAP

Once you can read the basic features of the map, you need to understand the other information that it can provide. The map can give you distance from one point to another, as well as show you the differences between what your compass is reading (called magnetic north) and what the map has laid out (called grid north). The slight variation is called the declination and will be important if you plan to travel using your map to obtain bearings.

For rudimentary navigation, you do not need to worry much about the declination differences between grid north and magnetic north. However, if you are trying to be very precise over distance and intend to take your bearings from the map, you will need to understand this process. Your map contains a declination diagram, which will show you the amount of degree offset left or right between magnetic north and map north. The top of any map is oriented north. Think of straight up on the map as corresponding to the hands of a clock pointing to 12. Magnetic north is actually left or right of 12 o'clock, depending on where you are standing on the earth's surface. Your compass always points to magnetic north, but the map is made to linear and lateral direction, so north on the map is not magnetic north. This difference is indicated in the declination diagram as a degree of offset. Once you find the declination diagram, you can set the declination difference in your compass

if it has adjustable declination or use the calculation based on the degree of offset on every bearing you take from the map when planning your route. See **FIGURE 7.22** for an example of a declination diagram on a map.

DECLINATION DIAGRAM ON A MAP

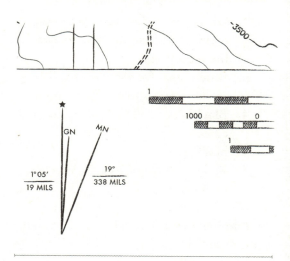

Figure 7.22

Orienting the map allows you to match the two-dimensional image on the map to what you're seeing in the landscape. To orient the map, place your open compass on one corner so the straight edge of your compass and the grid lines on the map are parallel. If you are using this map to figure a route and to factor travel bearings, to start this operation you will need to either have the declination difference set on the compass or offset your bezel ring that amount from 360 degrees at the top of the compass. When you've done this, rotate the map until the north needle is again in the doghouse. The map will be oriented to the terrain in front of you. Make sure that when you begin this procedure your map compass top is toward the top of the map. See **FIGURE 7.23** for an example of how to orient the map.

ORIENTING THE MAP

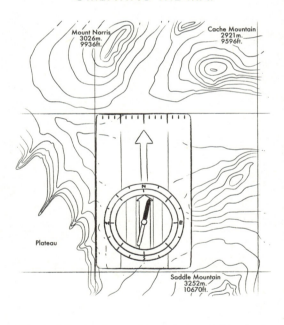

Figure 7.23

You may determine that your destination is two kilometers (klicks) ahead but once you start walking you'll need to keep track of how far you've gone. Pace beads are used to measure distance traveled. Simply create two strings of beads: one strand of nine beads and one strand of four beads. These are used to count five kilometers. Each bead on the side with nine beads represents 100 meters, and each bead on the side with four beads represents one kilometer. You will start with all beads at the top of the two strings, and drop beads accordingly as you travel in 100-meter increments. The key to this is figuring how many paces it takes to walk 100 meters. Keep track in your camp journal or notes of your pace in various terrains carrying your typical gear. Over time you will be able to determine your average pace. See **FIGURE 7.24** for an example of pace beads.

PACE BEADS

Figure 7.24

CHAPTER 8

HUNTING, FISHING, AND TRAPPING

TO HUNT OR trap an animal, you have to know where they eat, where they live, and where they travel. Animals are predictable. They usually travel the same routes, and this makes it easy to learn their patterns.

Understanding what animals eat, which may differ depending on the time of year, will allow you to seek food sources and then look for sign. It is often easier to find a large patch of berries than a small animal track, especially at a distance. The water's edge is a great place to start. There, it should be very easy to find not only smaller food items but also the prey of the larger animals as well.

— ANIMAL SIGN —

Animal sign is anything the animal leaves as a trace that indicates it may have passed through the area. It is the key to eliminating guesswork when hunting or trapping. Only hunt or trap where there is sign. Tracks and scat are two types of sign animals leave behind. See **FIGURES 8.1 AND 8.2** for examples of animal tracks and scat. Keep in mind that tracks may not appear as shown due to many factors, including weather, age of the track, the conditions of the ground when the track was left, and more.

DIFFERENT TYPES OF ANIMAL TRACKS

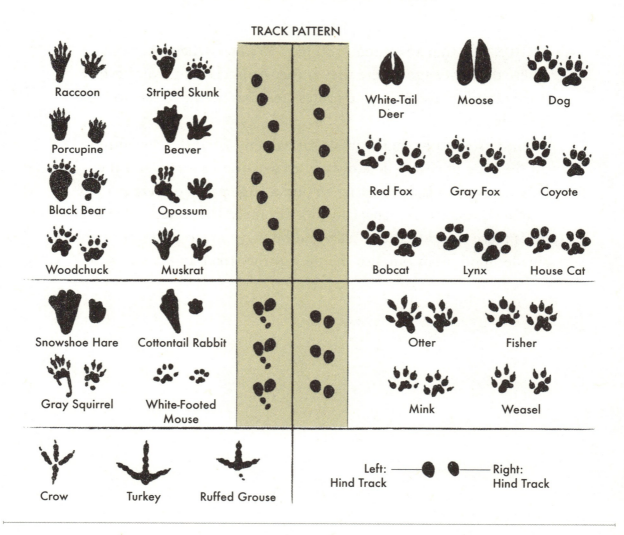

Figure 8.1

BUSHCRAFT ILLUSTRATED

DIFFERENT TYPES OF ANIMAL SCAT

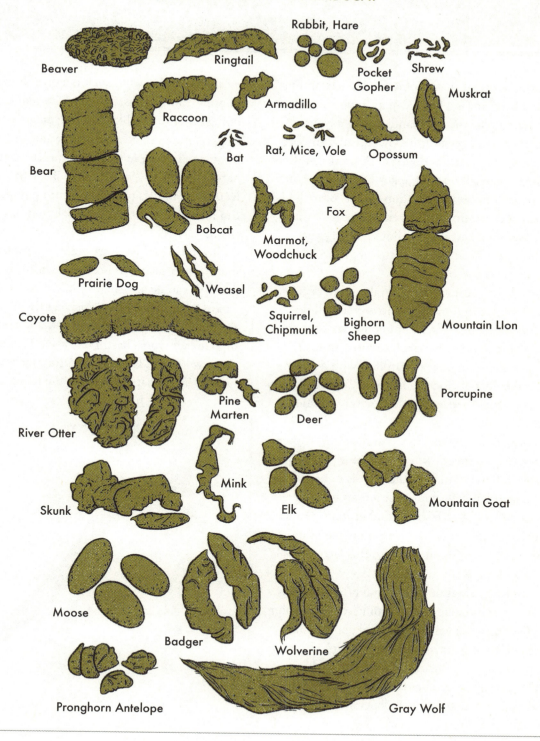

Figure 8.2

— HUNTING —

Hunting is an art in and of itself. Understanding animal behavior is a key element, but understanding how to play the wind and to take advantage of natural camouflage and shadows are also important. Anything you can do to break up the outlines of the human silhouette are key here. Scent control is also important: you don't want to smell like an urban environment. Extremes in any of these cases are not a necessity as thousands of game animals have been killed by hunters wearing red flannel shirts and blue jeans.

The key to scent control is taken care of for you if you are in hunting camp as you will be around the smoke of a campfire much of the time. This is not an offensive smell to most animals as it is something they are familiar with already. Natural colors of clothing are best although many animals cannot see colors well anyway, excluding birds.

One of the best tactics when hunting—other than trying to stay downwind of your prey on approach (either yours or theirs)—is to be still. Movement will give your position away faster than anything else. To be a good ground hunter you must realize this. The reason people hunt from an elevated stand is due to this fact: animals rarely look up when walking.

Hunting in stationary, natural ground blinds from a transition area like a trail between bedding and feeding areas will always yield good results once you have scouted the area for sign. Hunting weapons are not difficult to make from what you can find in the natural environment, although what you choose to use will depend on the prey you intend to hunt.

A simple throwing stick is a great hunting tool of opportunity to use while you're walking and doing other things like scouting an area or setting traps. Animals in and near the water can also be hunted with simple tools that can be made from natural materials. See **FIGURES 8.3 THROUGH 8.10** for examples of simple hunting tools you can make from natural materials and how to use them.

To start, a rabbit stick is a very simple device made for throwing in horizontal fashion at small game. It can be any shape you desire; however, I have found that something slightly bent, about the length of your arm pit to fist, and about 1.5" in diameter works best. Hardwood is best and green wood will last well if hitting rocks and hard ground if you happen to miss the target.

RABBIT STICK

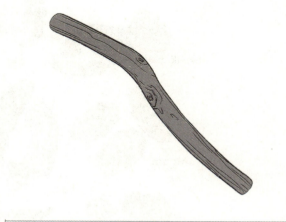

Figure 8.3

THROWING A RABBIT STICK

Figure 8.4

Bundle bows are literally made from a bundle of sticks. It is best to use three green sticks for this, each about 1" in diameter, with two opposing with the thinner end as the knock point. They will be staked in a pyramid fashion with the third shorter piece a bit over one-third the length of the two main sticks toward the belly to add strength.

Bushcraft Tip

If you haven't hunted or trapped before, think small. Keep your expectations to a minimum, and don't think you need to buy every possible gear item to succeed.

BUNDLE BOW

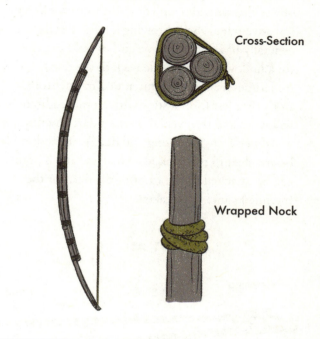

Cross-Section

Wrapped Nock

Figure 8.5

BUNDLE BOW KNOTS

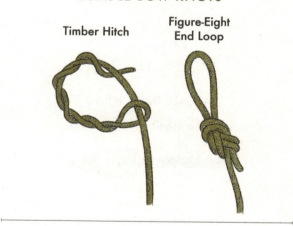

Timber Hitch

Figure-Eight End Loop

Figure 8.6

An atlatl, a spear or dart thrower, is a simple object that provides a pivot point to gain mechanical advantage when throwing a long thin dart. It generally has a spur on one end to hold the dart (in a hollowed area on the back of the dart), and sometimes has a weight for added momentum. In its simplest form a stick with a pointed branch will work as a thrower. To make a dart any flexible wood between 5'–7' long will do. Feathers should be attached to the back like an arrow and a point can be attached to the front of the dart for the intended game to be taken.

ATLATL

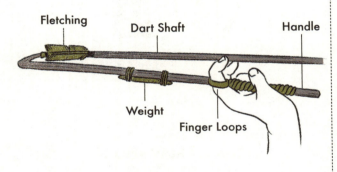

Figure 8.7

ATLATL DART HEAD

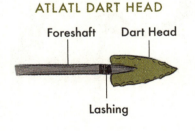

Figure 8.8

USING AN ATLATL

Figure 8.9

A bola is simply three cords with weights of some sort on the end all attached together at the non-weighted end with a knot. This can then be twirled around in the air and thrown toward a target to either wrap the legs of something large or incapacitate something smaller by blunt force trauma.

BOLA

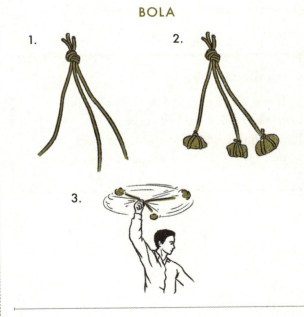

Figure 8.10

— TRAPPING —

Traps usually perform one of four main functions: live capture, strangle, mangle, or dangle. Almost all traps contain three major components: the trigger, the lever, and the engine. The biggest advantage to primitive trapping, when you make your own traps from natural materials you find in the woods, is that it takes a lot less gear carried to accomplish, and setup time is minimal once you own the skills.

Trapping for food should be thought about in small scale since micro-trapping is really where you can have great success. It may not be so appealing to think about eating smaller animals like chipmunks, rats, and squirrels, but these traps are less labor intensive to build and can be made using relatively little amounts of cordage. Deadfall traps work well for micro-trapping and cage-type traps will be successful on birds as well. You'll learn about these and other primitive traps in the following sections.

Traps have to be adapted to location, target species, and weather. The art of trapping takes years to perfect but learning a few simple triggers and trap systems will give you a good start in the learning experience. I have found simple is always best.

Bushcraft Tip

Don't wait until you are hungry to secure food; this will only make things worse and lessen the chance for success. Just like anything else, hunting, fishing, and trapping use calories and energy. If you wait till the tank is empty, you won't have the resources to make your hunting efficient. One of the greatest benefits to attempting to find food in the wild is the fact that it occupies the mind. This can work wonders in times of waiting in an SAR (Search and Rescue) scenario.

The most important thing to learn in simple primitive trapping is one trigger system that can be adapted to many traps. In this way, you can make several and adjust triggers and traps on the fly to fit the situation. Any trigger on a trap is the portion or component that releases tension and springs the trap. Many times this will be a combination of two or more components involving a level and fulcrum of sorts, as seen in the following illustrations. See **FIGURES 8.11 AND 8.12** for examples of triggers.

L7 TRIGGER

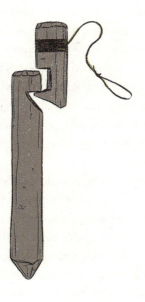

Figure 8.12

PROMONTORY PEG TRIGGER

Figure 8.11

Bushcraft Tip

All states require hunters to take hunter-training classes, so don't be surprised if you're asked to show proof that you've fulfilled this requirement before you're allowed the necessary hunting licenses and permits.

Snare traps are nooses that catch small animals, usually around the neck or body. **FIGURES 8.13 THROUGH 8.16** show examples of snares. Note that for larger game a thicker diameter material is needed for added tensile strength.

CORDAGE SNARE LOOP

Figure 8.13

TREADLE SNARE

Figure 8.14

POWERED SNARE

Figure 8.15

BIRD SNARE

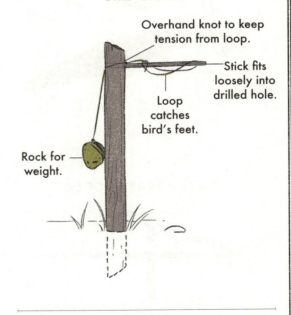

Overhand knot to keep tension from loop.

Stick fits loosely into drilled hole.

Loop catches bird's feet.

Rock for weight.

Figure 8.16

DEADFALL TRAPS

Deadfall traps can be used with the same trigger systems used for snare traps. Deadfall traps are used to crush/suffocate an animal by weight and need to be five times heavier than the weight of the prey to be killed; the trap will crush the prey. Triggers that release the weight are a matter of preference for the type of trap used and the size of the game, but all components should be matched to the intended prey in size. **FIGURES 8.17 THROUGH 8.23** show examples of deadfall traps.

FIGURE 4 DEADFALL TRAP

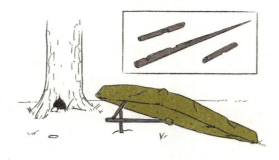

Figure 8.17

FIGURE 4 TRAP TRIGGER

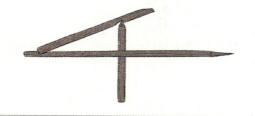

Figure 8.18

PIUTE DEADFALL TRAP

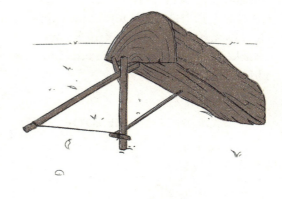

Figure 8.19

PIUTE DEADFALL TRAP TRIGGER

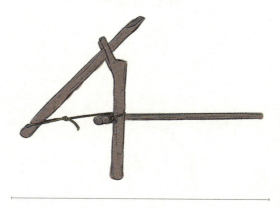

Figure 8.20

SIMPLE LOG DEADFALL TRAP

Figure 8.21

FLIP TRIGGER DEADFALL TRAP

Figure 8.22

SWEEPING DEADFALL TRAP

Figure 8.23

Bushcraft Tip

The difference between baits and lures is simple: a lure attracts the animal by smell to the set location, and bait is something the animal wants to eat or investigate. Lures are usually made of glands or oils, and bait is usually food-based. A good example of lure is skunk musk; it can bring animals in for a look from a very long distance. Bait consists of things such as raw meat.

Snares and deadfall traps aren't the only way you can catch small animals. A variety of other types of traps can be made from natural materials. See **FIGURES 8.24 THROUGH 8.28** for examples of more types of traps.

CLAP BOW TRAP

Figure 8.24

CLAP BOW CLOSE-UP

Figure 8.25

WINDLASS TRAP

Figure 8.26

Bushcraft Tip

Many people overcomplicate primitive trapping! Trapping is very simple to understand. Any trap that effectively holds or kills an animal is all you need. I have traveled all over the world, and tribal people who are still hunter-gathers have shown me that simple traps employing a simple toggle trigger are the best all-around trap to use for securing meat, and the ones they use every day for small mammals and birds. The KISS (Keep It Simple and Sensible) method works for trapping.

RAT TRAP

Figure 8.27

NET TRAP FOR MAMMALS

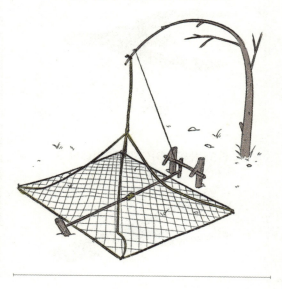

Figure 8.28

BIRD TRAPPING

Cage traps can be used to catch the bird alive, conserving it for later use. Cage traps work well for ground-dwelling birds such as quail, grouse, and pheasant. They can also be used for small perching species such as mourning doves and turtledoves. **FIGURE 8.29** is an example of a cage trap for catching birds.

BIRD CAGE TRAP

Figure 8.29

— FISHING —

It is my opinion that survival begins on the water's edge. Everything needs water and many animals either live in or hunt near water for their food as well. Fishing is one of the easiest ways to easily obtain food and is great fun to do the old way with stick poles and hand lines. Nets are also fun to make and great to use as well where they are permitted. Just like many bushcraft projects things like nets are very cordage intensive, and it may be best to practice these skills with cordage you have brought just for this purpose.

Carving the needles and gauges is a great way to practice your crafting skills along the way. (The needle or shuttle is what holds the net line and is used to create the knot; the gauge is what determines the size of the individual mesh, which must be matched to the size fish you are looking to catch.) Making things like spears or gigs is very useful not only for fishing near the bank or in shallow water, but also for catching frogs, which can be easy to obtain in the proper season and make a good meal.

SPEAR OR GIG

The spear or gig is a simple tool that you can use for fishing. See **FIGURES 8.30 THROUGH 8.32** for examples of gigs.

FISHING GIG, VERSION 1

Figure 8.30

FISHING GIG, VERSION 2

Figure 8.31

FISHING GIG, VERSION 3

Figure 8.32

BUSHCRAFT ILLUSTRATED

FISHING RODS

You can use a simple wooden pole, line made of cordage, and a hook scavenged or carved from natural materials or fashioned from materials you've brought with you into the woods to create a fishing rod. Hooks like traps or nets must be sized toward the intended fish to be caught; erring toward smaller is better. See **FIGURES 8.33 AND 8.34** for examples of fish hooks.

FISH HOOKS, SET 1

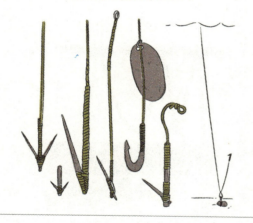

Figure 8.33

FISH HOOKS, SET 2

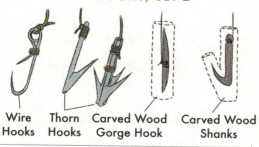

| Wire Hooks | Thorn Hooks | Carved Wood Gorge Hook | Carved Wood Shanks |

Figure 8.34

FISHING WEIR

You can use a weir, an enclosure made of sticks or stones set in low water, to catch fish as well. See **FIGURE 8.35** for an example of a stone weir.

STONE WEIR

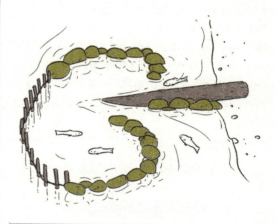

Figure 8.35

Bushcraft Tip

A line ladder is a miniature ladder that holds the rigged lines neatly. They can be easily fashioned from a flat strip of wood carved into a half-moon shape on each end. The length is a matter of personal preference; I like mine about 4" long. Wrap the line around them to keep it neat for use and set up for that particular application.

NETS AND BASKETS FOR TRAPPING

To trap fish and other water-loving animals, you can use nets and baskets. You can make nets of any shape, size, or dimension to fit your needs. A good dip net is simple to make and easy to use. Nets can also cover and haul cargo or be used in land traps when capturing live food.

You can use natural materials to make a net needle and the cordage you'll need to use to make the net (see Chapter 3 for more on cordage and knots). **FIGURES 8.36 THROUGH 8.39** show a wooden net needle and various examples of net shuttles.

WOODEN NET NEEDLE

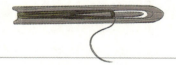

Figure 8.36

NET SHUTTLE, VERSION 1

Figure 8.37

NET SHUTTLE, VERSION 2

Figure 8.38

NET SHUTTLE, VERSION 3

Figure 8.39

FIGURES 8.40 THROUGH 8.43 show various net knots and net-tying techniques.

NET KNOT

Figure 8.40

SIMPLE NET

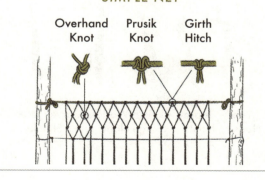

Figure 8.41

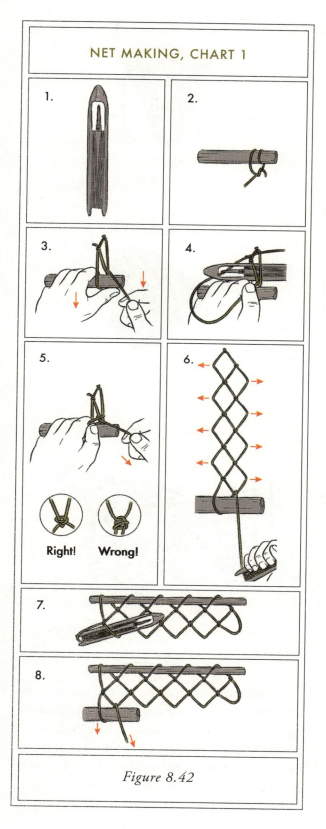

NET MAKING, CHART 1

1.

2.

3.

4.

5.

Right!   Wrong!

6.

7.

8.

Figure 8.42

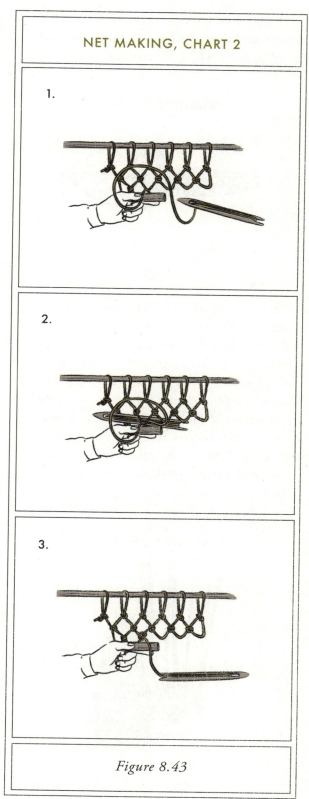

NET MAKING, CHART 2

1.

2.

3.

Figure 8.43

FIGURE 8.44 shows a primitive dip net that's been created using the net needles and techniques shown in the previous illustrations.

PRIMITIVE DIP NET

Figure 8.44

You can weave baskets for trapping in any material such as vines, bark, or splits. Weave in and out of the splits. You can start to shape this weave into a basket by gradually lifting the sides and controlling the tightness of the weave to form a round container. Finish this off by wrapping another piece of the material in an overhand running-stitch fashion around the top and trim any excess sticks or twigs off the finished product.

See FIGURES 8.45 THROUGH 8.48 for examples of baskets for trapping fish.

MAKING FISH TRAPS

Figure 8.45

DIP NET BASKET

Figure 8.46

BASKET FISH TRAP

Figure 8.47

BASKET WEIR

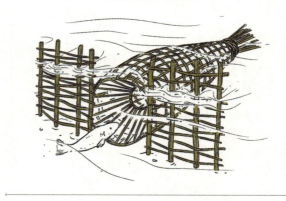

Figure 8.48

Basket traps are made like normal baskets with a bit less attention to neatness. They are all based on stakes and weavers; the stakes give the basket rigidity and the weavers give the basket structure. In simplest form a basket will have an odd number of stakes, so the weavers can be wound in behind and in front of every other stake.

CHAPTER 9

PROCESSING GAME

BUSHCRAFT INCLUDES MAKING the implements it takes to catch our food as well as to prepare or keep the food from spoiling. In this chapter, you'll learn how to process the game you've trapped or otherwise captured.

— DEALING WITH LIVE FOOD —

Remember, "Live food never spoils." If you do not want to have to immediately process the food you have harvested you should attempt to catch it alive if possible. Live food can be kept easily enough if it is watered and possibly fed something depending on the duration in captivity. Many domesticated animals started out as live food penned up for later use. Fish and most water animals can be kept in baskets right in the water as long as the rim is above the water line.

If you intend to eat the food immediately it is much easier to have it dispatched by the capture method to dispense with that chore. You should think right away how much you can actually eat in a single day as in warm weather food can spoil unless it is preserved, making another step necessary if you want to prolong the use of it. For these reasons it is best to become highly skilled at capturing or harvesting animals that can be processed, cooked, and consumed in a single day, unless you are attempting some longer-term living arrangement.

Bushcraft Tip

There are many food sources that fall into the category of live game, including:

- Fish
- Frogs
- Turtles
- Small mammals
- Birds
- Eggs

These food sources are fairly easily hunted, trapped, and caught so you have no real need to worry about larger game.

PROCESSING YOUR CATCH

Once you have secured your game by using the methods outlined in Chapter 8, you need to first remove the guts so that the meat does not begin to rot. With fish, the gills must also be removed. Once you have done this it is considered field dressed. You can then further process the game by either quartering in the case of animals, and then even going as far as boning or removing the meat from the bones for ease of cooking and use, or in the case of fish filleting them. All types of game are a bit different, but the types of animals—fish, mammals, birds, etc.—will be very similar in process.

See **FIGURES 9.1 AND 9.2** for examples of field tool sets that aid in butchering game.

FIELD PROCESSING TOOL SET

Figure 9.2

FIGURE 9.3 is an example of an old-fashioned hickory butcher knife.

BUTCHER KNIFE

Figure 9.3

POCKET GAME PROCESSING TOOL

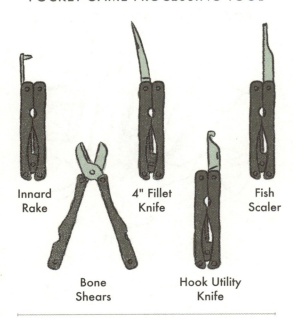

Innard Rake

4" Fillet Knife

Fish Scaler

Bone Shears

Hook Utility Knife

Figure 9.1

Smaller mammals such as ground squirrels, mice, rats, and the like can be processed by making a shallow slice to remove guts and anal tract, then placing the animal in the fire to burn the fur off and cook the meat. Or, you can skin them with a knife. Remember that any leftover meat should be used for baiting a trap to catch something else. **FIGURES 9.4 THROUGH 9.9** show the steps to processing a squirrel. This method is used for most mammals with the skin being removed in different ways depending on the type and size of the animal.

PROCESSING A SQUIRREL, STEP 1

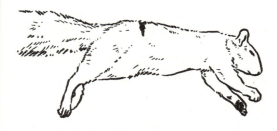

Figure 9.4

▲ Make a lateral cut two-thirds of the way down the back.

PROCESSING A SQUIRREL, STEP 2

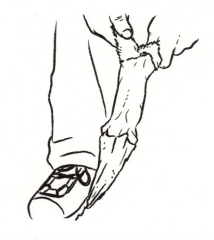

Figure 9.5

▲ Insert fingers and strip off the skin.

PROCESSING A SQUIRREL, STEP 3

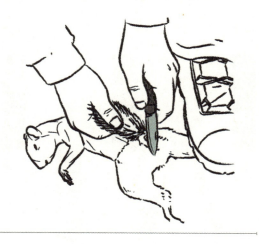

Figure 9.6

▲ Cut off head and tail.

PROCESSING A SQUIRREL, STEP 4

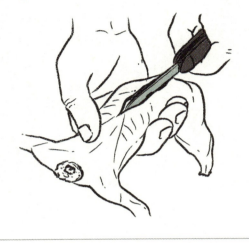

Figure 9.7

▲ Open gut cavity carefully and shallowly so you don't puncture any organs.

PROCESSING A SQUIRREL, STEP 5

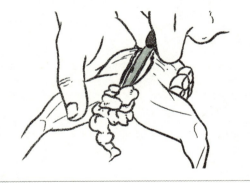

Figure 9.8

▲ Remove the guts leaving the intestines attached at the anus, and cut around the bung to remove without damaging.

PROCESSING A SQUIRREL, STEP 6

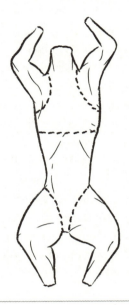

Figure 9.9

▲ The animal can now be spit cooked or processed further by quartering.

Bushcraft Tip

I use some type of food-grade oil on my tools all the time in case I am going to process food with them. The oil protects the tools from rust; using food-grade oil means I won't ingest anything toxic. In salt-water environments stainless steel is best but I find carbon much easier to maintain in the field.

Field dressing is the beginning process to preserve the meat by removing the guts to keep the meat from going bad. It is also a good idea to cool the inside cavity as fast as possible by immersing in a cold creek or packing with snow.

Medium-sized critters are not much more difficult to handle than small game. The biggest chore is removing the fur. Quarter them for quicker cooking. Remove all innards and the anal tract. Be careful not to perforate the gut or intestines while removing them, as this can foul the taste of the meat. Many innards are worth consuming, such as the heart and liver. Check the organs of any kill to ensure that they look healthy: brightly colored with no blotching or worms. Again, remember to use leftovers for several traps or fishing. See **FIGURES 9.10 THROUGH 9.15** for steps to skinning a rabbit. **FIGURE 9.16** shows how to do this process without using a knife.

SKINNING A RABBIT, STEP 1

Figure 9.10

SKINNING A RABBIT, STEP 2

Figure 9.11

SKINNING A RABBIT, STEP 3

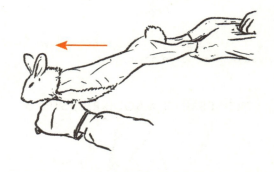

Figure 9.12

FIGURE 9.13 shows knife cuts for skinning.

KNIFE CUTS FOR SKINNING

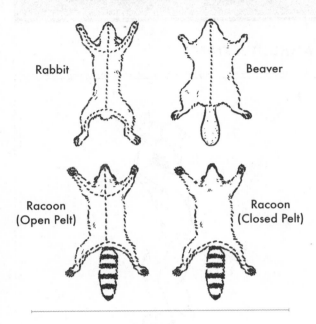

Rabbit

Beaver

Racoon
(Open Pelt)

Racoon
(Closed Pelt)

Figure 9.13

Bushcraft Tip

Skunk scent is one of the best long-distance call lures. Skunks that are killed then bagged in a drum liner can be used to contaminate other items with scent.

FIGURE 9.14 shows how to remove a rabbit's head after skinning.

REMOVING A RABBIT'S HEAD

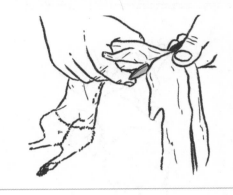

Figure 9.14

FIGURE 9.15 shows how to remove a rabbit's extremities prior to field dressing.

REMOVAL OF EXTREMITIES

Figure 9.15

GUTTING A RABBIT WITHOUT A KNIFE

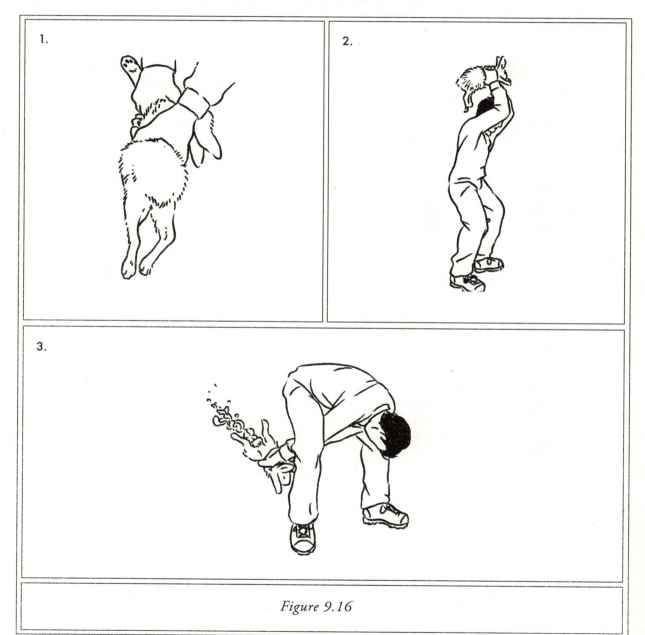

Figure 9.16

FIGURES 9.17 THROUGH 9.19 show how to open the gut cavity, remove the guts, and find the scent glands on medium and large game. Note that there is no real set moment to remove the head of an animal and it may not be necessary at all if you are boning the meat. But it is usually done on small game along with the feet before removing the skin, unless you are trying to preserve the hide and case skinning the animal.

GUT REMOVAL ON MEDIUM GAME

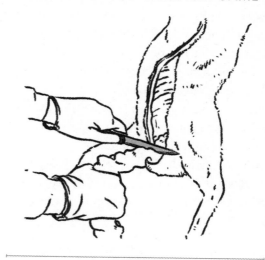

Figure 9.18

OPENING THE GUT CAVITY ON MEDIUM AND LARGE HANGING GAME

Figure 9.17

LOCATION OF SCENT GLANDS

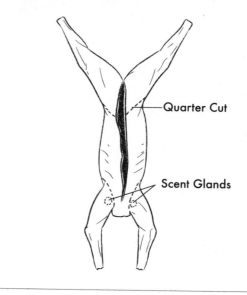

Quarter Cut

Scent Glands

Figure 9.19

Process fish by slitting them from the vent or anus to the base of the gills, removing all guts, and tearing out the gills. You can scale the fish or just cook it with the scales or skin on, and eat the meat from the inside out like a baked potato. If you choose to skin a catfish before eating, you will want a pair of pliers for scaling and skinning, as it can be tough. All freshwater fish in North America are edible. **FIGURE 9.20** shows an older Frosts fishing knife. **FIGURE 9.21** shows how to skin a catfish.

FROSTS FISHING KNIFE

Figure 9.20

SKINNING A CATFISH

1.

2.

3.

4.

Figure 9.21

FILLETING A FISH

When filleting you are essentially deboning the fish. After gutting, a cut is made across the pectoral fin, and the knife is used to cut along the spine and just outside the edge of the ribs. This flap is then laid to the opposite side and a fillet (flexible blade) knife is used to remove the skin from the opposite side, leaving only the backbone and ribs on completion. **FIGURE 9.22** shows how to fillet a fish.

FILLETING A FISH

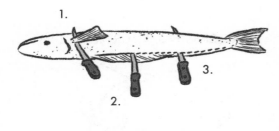
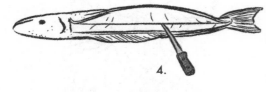

Figure 9.22

Removing or plucking the feathers off a bird in the wild can be a time-consuming process; you are better off skinning the bird as you would a mammal. The main thing to remember with birds is to empty the crop, a pouch at the base of the throat where food is held prior to digestion. This will usually contain dry seeds and such from recent feedings. See **FIGURE 9.23** for an example of how to field dress a game bird.

FIELD DRESSING A GAME BIRD

Figure 9.23

Reptiles such as snakes can be skinned and the guts removed, then cooked like any other food. Remove the head of any poisonous snake prior to processing. Frogs can also be skinned or just cooked and consumed after gutting.

Turtles are a bit tricky: cut the head off, hang the body upside down to bleed out, remove the lower shell by cutting the thin layer of membrane between the shell and the meat, and clean out the innards. You can use the shell as a pot in which to cook the meat. Turtle meat makes very good bait for fishing. **FIGURES 9.24 THROUGH 9.27** show you how to process a turtle.

PROCESSING A TURTLE, STEP 2

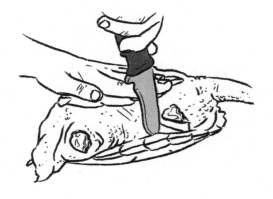

Figure 9.25

PROCESSING A TURTLE, STEP 1

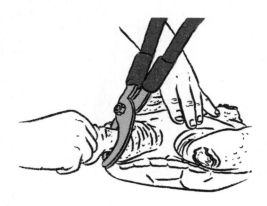

Figure 9.24

PROCESSING A TURTLE, STEP 3

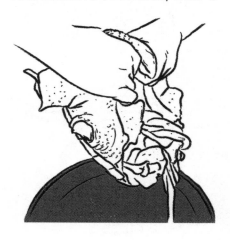

Figure 9.26

PROCESSING A TURTLE, STEP 4

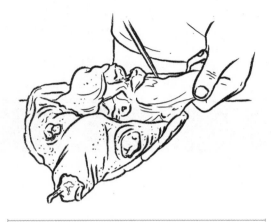

Figure 9.27

To process a crawfish before cooking, remove the mud vein by pulling the middle of the three tail fins away from the tail. The animal can be cooked as is at this point. Once done the tail can be cleanly removed by pulling it from the body and the tail meat consumed. See **FIGURE 9.28** for an example of how to process a crawfish.

Bushcraft Tip

When breaking down an animal, use the anatomical lines already in place to guide your knife. Cut along muscle groups (instead of through them) and between bones instead of trying to hack your way through.

PROCESSING A CRAWFISH

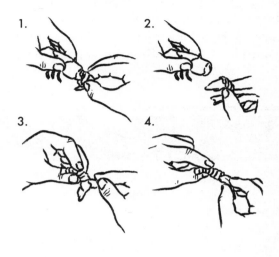

Figure 9.28

See **FIGURE 9.29** for an example of how to process a snake.

PROCESSING A SNAKE

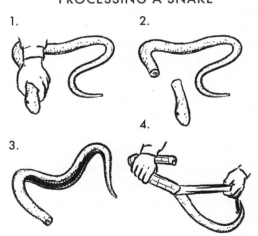

Figure 9.29

— PRESERVING MEAT —

There are a couple of simple ways you can preserve meat with little to no excess gear or additional resources. Preserving meat works the same with most animal species, but remember: bacteria is the enemy here, so the cooler the meat is kept or the sooner it is dried out or cooked the better.

DRYING

Drying removes moisture from the meat and makes it available for consumption later on a trip or on the trail. The key is to cut the meat as thin as possible so that the process happens quickly. You can dry meat by suspending it over a fire with low heat for a period of time until the meat cracks when bent, like jerky, or you can sun-dry the meat on a flat rock or rack. If a full hot sun is available, rotate the meat from side to side until dry. How long the drying process will take is dependent on many factors, including how thick/thin the meat is cut, but generally it is several hours to days. **FIGURE 9.30** shows an example of drying fish.

Bushcraft Tip
Remember that any items left from the butchering that you are not using can become bait for other meals and traps, as well as an attractant for hunting later.

DRYING FISH

Figure 9.30

To smoke meat, you will need an enclosure of some sort made from available gear such as a poncho, trash bag, space blanket, etc. It can also be made from natural material. The enclosure causes the smoke and heat to rise directly to the meat and accomplishes the smoking process. Unlike with drying, you are actually slow cooking the meat and not trying to remove all moisture. The smoke adds flavor as well as antibacterial properties to the meat. You can use green wood to aid in smoke content, but stay away from resinous woods such as pines. See **FIGURES 9.31 THROUGH 9.33** for examples of a pit smoker, a rack smoker, and a teepee smoker.

RACK SMOKER

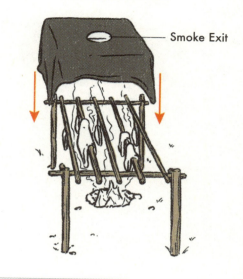

Smoke Exit

Figure 9.32

PIT SMOKER

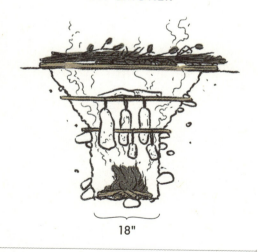

18"

Figure 9.31

TEEPEE SMOKER

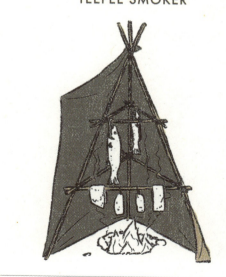

Figure 9.33

CHAPTER 10

PLANTS

IT IS IMPORTANT to realize that while you want to practice bushcraft and become familiar with local plants, including which ones are edible (and taste good!), you also have a responsibility to yourself to ensure correct identification and to others by not overharvesting in a single area. You should only harvest what you need. This may mean that you harvest only the young leaves and not the roots or bulbs or just the flowers and not the entire plant. You must become a steward of the land as well as a good bushcrafter. It is also important to research these plants as many may need to be processed a certain way or harvested at a certain time of year for best results and palatability. In this chapter you'll learn about foraging (gathering wild plants).

— WHAT IS FORAGING? —

Foraging is what you do when you harvest plants from the landscape—be they fruits, nuts, berries, or other plant materials—and consume them as food. It is a wonderful feeling to be able to understand which plants will make a fresh salad, others that may provide a seasoning for meat, and even some that can be made into a flour substitute for making flatbreads. Part of the connection to the land bushcrafters are striving for involves using all of its resources to our advantage, including its ability to provide food.

Bushcraft Tip

You don't have to learn about every wild plant in order to forage. Learn about the edibles in your area or where you like to camp. Local knowledge is what matters.

In addition, knowing some basic plant lore can keep you from wasting time. Nearly 100 percent of all white berries are toxic, for example; you don't need to bother finding out if the white-berried plant that grows in your local woods is edible. It probably isn't.

To make sure you're eating plants that won't hurt you, you need to be sure you have correctly identified the plant in question. A good rule of thumb taught by a popular forager known as Green Deane is to ITEMize plants.

- **Identification.** Identify the plant positively with several sources. If you misidentify a plant and eat it, you may get sick.
- **Time of year.** Is the plant growing in the proper time of year according to references? If it seems to be growing out of season, you may have misidentified the plant.
- **Environment.** Make sure the plant is growing in the proper environment. If a plant is supposed to like growing in dry areas and you find it in a wet, boggy spot, you may have the wrong plant.
- **Methods.** Understand the proper methods of harvest and preparation. With some plants, you can eat the leaves but not the stem, or vice versa. Sometimes the berries are poisonous but the foliage is not. Some plants can be eaten raw but others must be cooked before eating.

Spend time with someone else who has this knowledge as you are learning.

The illustrations in **FIGURES 10.1 THROUGH 10.30** show examples of commonly found plants that you can forage. Remember that every region has local plants that you will want to become familiar with as well.

AUTUMN OLIVE

Figure 10.1

BLACK WALNUT TREE

Figure 10.2

BLACK WALNUTS

Figure 10.3

BURDOCK PLANT

Figure 10.4

CATTAILS

Figure 10.6

BURDOCK ROOT, HARVESTED

Figure 10.5

CATTAIL ROOTS AND SHOOTS

Figure 10.7

CHICORY

Figure 10.8

CHOKECHERRY

Figure 10.9

DANDELION ROOT

Figure 10.10

ELDERBERRY

Figure 10.11

FIDDLEHEAD FERNS

Figure 10.12

HICKORY NUTS

Figure 10.13

HIGHBUSH CRANBERRIES

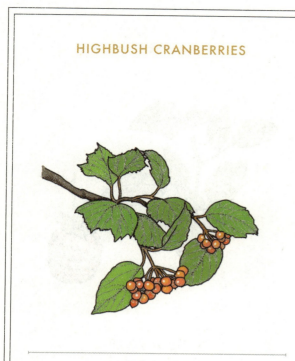

Figure 10.14

PAW PAW

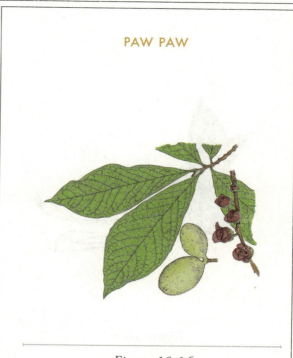

Figure 10.16

MULBERRY

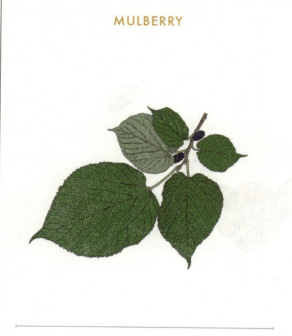

Figure 10.15

PEPPERGRASS

Figure 10.17

RAMPS

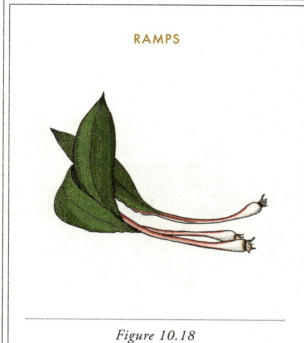

Figure 10.18

RASPBERRIES

Figure 10.19

RED PINE NUTS IN SHELL

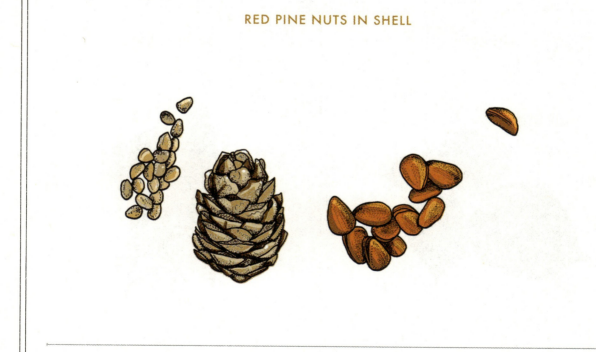

Figure 10.20

STAGHORN SUMAC

Figure 10.21

WATERCRESS

Figure 10.23

SWAMP VIOLET

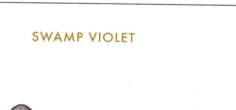

Figure 10.22

WHITE OAK ACORNS

Figure 10.24

WILD GRAPES

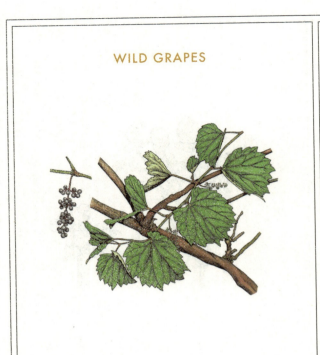

Figure 10.25

WILD LETTUCE

Figure 10.26

WILD ONION

Figure 10.27

WILD STRAWBERRIES

Figure 10.28

WINTER CRESS

Figure 10.29

WOOD SORREL

Figure 10.30

— OTHER PLANTS TO KNOW —

In addition to foraging for plants to eat, you'll look for plants to use in different ways as well. **FIGURES 10.31 THROUGH 10.34** show a variety of plants that will be useful to you in the woods along with some information that tells you what they can be used for.

HONEYSUCKLE

Figure 10.31

▲ Used for cordage. See Chapter 3.

QUEEN OF THE MEADOW

Figure 10.33

▲ Used as a tinder source. See Chapter 6.

MILKWEED OVUM

Figure 10.32

▲ Used as a tinder source. See Chapter 6.

VIRGINIA CREEPER

Figure 10.34

▲ Used for cordage. See Chapter 3.

CHAPTER 11

FIRST AID

I APPROACH FIRST AID from the perspective of bushcraft. That doesn't mean you should not carry a first aid kit. It simply means you should understand how to use material from the landscape to enhance or supplement what you've carried in. When in the wild, you have to think in terms of self-care—how to take care of injuries to yourself—as well as helping others in your group should they be injured. In this chapter, you'll learn how to do all this and more.

— THE FIVE Bs OF FIRST AID —

When enjoying the outdoors, the most common injuries are the Five Bs:

1. Bleeding
2. Breaks, sprains, and strains
3. Blisters
4. Burns
5. Bites and stings

Being prepared to deal with these issues will help ensure a better outdoor experience.

Bushcraft Tip

Pour out 1 cup, 1 liter, and 2 liters of colored water on your driveway, then on the ground to become familiar with blood loss amounts and what they look like. Your body likely has between 4.5 and 5.5 liters of blood. Lose a quarter of it, and you could die.

BLEEDING

Cutting yourself (either in minor or more serious ways) is common when using tools. Understanding how to control bleeding can be very important.

STOP THE BLEEDING

The first step whenever you or someone else gets cut is to stop the bleeding. To do this, apply direct pressure. Don't place your bare hands directly on a cut or wound. Use gloves or another barrier that the blood can't get through, such as plastic bags or a Mylar blanket. Obviously if you are treating yourself, this is less important. See **FIGURE 11.1** for an example of applying direct pressure to a wound.

APPLYING DIRECT PRESSURE TO A WOUND

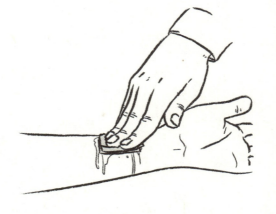

Figure 11.1

PRESSURE POINTS A pressure point is a place on the body where an artery can be pressed against a bone to slow bleeding. Find a place above the wound where you can feel a pulse. Apply pressure to that point to reduce bleeding. Some of these points are found in the neck (the carotid artery), at the end of the wrist, in the bend of the elbows, under the arm, and at the top of the thigh in the groin. See **FIGURE 11.2** for a chart of pressure points on the human body.

PRESSURE POINTS USED TO SLOW BLEEDING

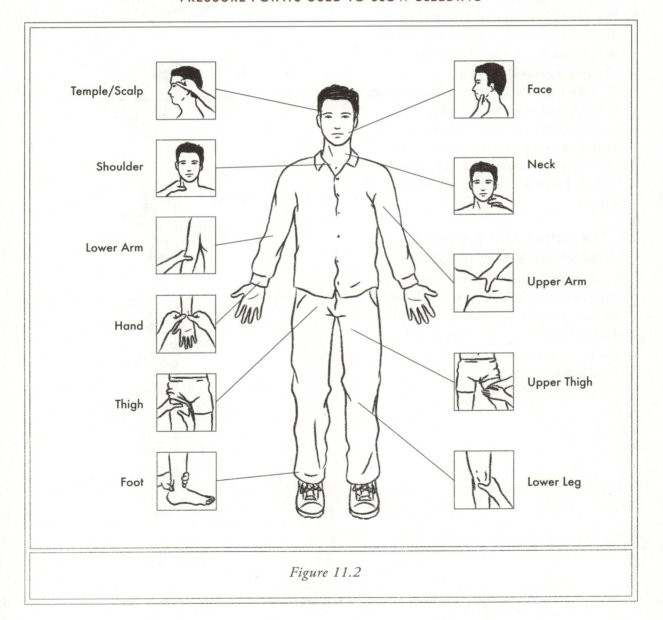

Figure 11.2

WOUND CLEANING AND BANDAGING

If the wound is very large or very deep or if debris is deeply imbedded, stop the bleeding but don't try to clean it. Seek medical attention immediately. Otherwise, brush away any dirt or debris or pluck it out with tweezers or a needle (clean the item by heating it with a lighter first and allowing it to cool).

Then flood the area with a large amount of clean, cool water to flush away any remaining dirt or debris. Use soap to wash around the wounded area, but don't try to get it into the wound itself. Then bandage it, and change the bandage at least once a day.

CREATING AND APPLYING BANDAGES AND DRESSINGS

To make a bandage in the wild, you can use gauze, Gorilla Tape, or tear strips of cloth from a piece of clothing. See **FIGURES 11.3 THROUGH 11.7** for examples of bandaging various body parts with an improvised bandage.

FOOT BANDAGING

1.
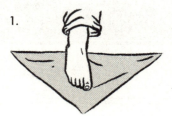

2.

3.

4.

5.
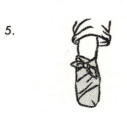

Figure 11.3

HAND BANDAGING

1.

2.
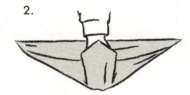

3.
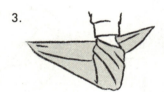

4.

5.

Figure 11.4

KNEE BANDAGING

1.

2.
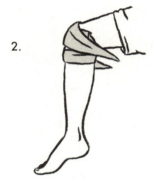

3.
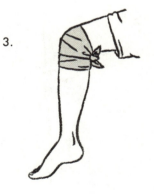

Figure 11.5

LEG BANDAGING

1.

2.

3.

Figure 11.6

PALM BANDAGING

1.

2.

3.

4.

5.

6.

Figure 11.7

USING TOURNIQUETS

A tourniquet is a bandage or other device that compresses a limb and its blood vessels in order to reduce blood flow. The tourniquet should be approximately 2" wide and a few layers thick. Never use rope or wire. Belts usually can't be tied tightly enough. Use a strip of cloth, a pack strap, a plastic drum liner, or something similar. The use of a tourniquet is a last resort and in fact is rarely needed. Improper application of a tourniquet may cause permanent damage to the tissues of the affected limb, leading to dire consequences such as amputation. However, if you or the patient are losing a lot of blood you should use a tourniquet.

Place the tourniquet 2" above the injury (or 2" above the joint if the injury is near a joint). Wrap the area with the tourniquet material. As you tighten the tourniquet, watch for the bleeding to stop. Once it does, stop tightening. Leave the tourniquet on until you can get professional help, since you don't want to loosen clots. These can get into the bloodstream and cause considerable damage. See **FIGURE 11.8** for an example of how to use a tourniquet.

USING A TOURNIQUET

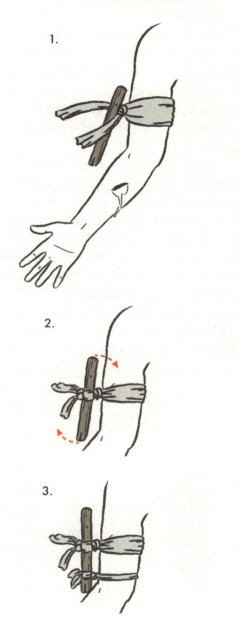

1.

2.

3.

Figure 11.8

NATURAL METHODS TO STOP BLEEDING

From the environment you can use astringent plants, like ash, to stop minor bleeding in areas that may bleed a lot even from a shallow cut such as the face, scalp, or fingers. Pine sap is a good, quick, new-skin-type covering and is also antiseptic in nature.

Many plants, like mullein, have large absorbent leaves for bandaging, and cat-tail fluff is also very absorbent. Plants like goldenrod and yarrow are also used traditionally to stop bleeding and can be found during at least three seasons in most of the Eastern Woodlands along open area edges like fields. White pine bark is also a great small natural bandage that has both a sticky effect and antiseptic properties. See **FIGURES 11.9 THROUGH 11.11** for examples of white pine, yarrow, and goldenrod.

YARROW

Figure 11.10

WHITE PINE

Figure 11.9

GOLDENROD

Figure 11.11

Whether you have a break, sprain, or strain, depending on severity, immobilization of the injured area may be key to being able to at least move (in the case of an ankle or leg injury). Many stiff materials from split limbs to heavy tree barks can be used for splinting materials, and a good Y-shaped stick will work as a makeshift crutch. Fingers can be splinted with many inner bark materials as well. See **FIGURES 11.12 THROUGH 11.17** for examples of how to improvise splints and slings from various materials for breaks, sprains, and strains.

You can also fashion a splint using the following pack items:

- Cargo tape
- Cordage
- Cutting tool
- Emergency blanket (this can also be fashioned into a sling)

Bushcraft Tip

The National Institutes of Health reports that about 70 percent of all nonfatal wilderness injuries are breaks, sprains, and strains. Make sure you have appropriate footwear, and don't be in a rush when conditions are wet or otherwise dangerous. Don't hike in the dark, and do ankle- and knee-strengthening exercises before you set out.

BLANKET SPLINTS

1.

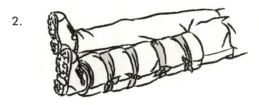

2.

3.

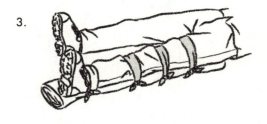

Figure 11.12

LEG SPLINT

Long Splint

Short Splint

Ankle Wrap

Twisting Stick

Cross Member

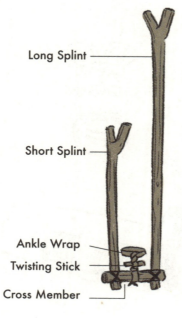

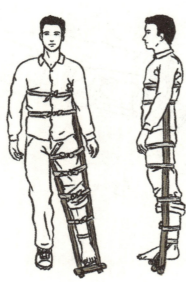

Figure 11.13

ARM SLING

1.

2.

3.

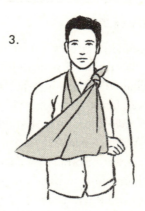

Figure 11.14

ELBOW SPLINT, BENT

Figure 11.15

ELBOW SPLINT, STRAIGHT

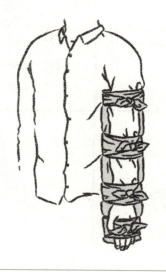

Figure 11.16

WRIST AND FOREARM SPLINT

Figure 11.17

Anything that will get the job done to splint an injured area is fine, so long as it does not pose risk of further injury. For comfort and protection, take padding and pack it around the splint wherever it seems loose. If you use natural materials for either the splint or its padding, do your best to keep dirt away from the wound itself and maintain a clean dressing. See **FIGURES 11.18 AND 11.19** for examples of how to pad a splint.

MAKING A PADDED SPLINT

1.

2.

3.

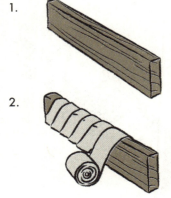

Figure 11.18

USING A PADDED SPLINT

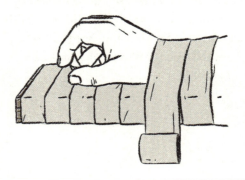

Figure 11.19

CARING FOR SPRAINS AND STRAINS

For any damage to a joint or muscle, once you've immobilized the injured area using the methods given in the previous section, keep the RICE procedure in mind:

- **R**est
- **I**ce
- **C**ompression
- **E**levation

See **FIGURE 11.20** for an example of RICE in action.

USING THE RICE SYSTEM TO TREAT SPRAINS AND STRAINS

Figure 11.20

Blisters are one of the most common injuries that you may encounter in the wild. They are caused by the rubbing of skin. The layers of your skin separate and in between the two layers, fluid accumulates, making the outer layer bulge. See **FIGURE 11.21** for an example of how blisters form.

HOW BLISTERS FORM

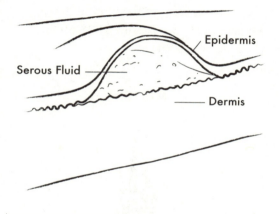

Figure 11.21

PREVENT BLISTERS

Reducing rubbing (friction) will reduce the likelihood of getting blisters. Make sure your boots fit properly. If they rub, add padding. You can also wear two pairs of socks to keep your feet from sliding in your boots.

On your hands, blisters are likely to occur when you're using a tool repeatedly, such as digging with a shovel. Wear gloves and treat hot spots by covering them with duct tape, moleskin, or another type of dressing.

TREAT BLISTERS

To treat blisters, take the following steps:

- Use clean water to flush the area.
- Clean the blade of your knife or a needle if you have one. You can use rubbing alcohol to do this. Or heat it with a flame and let it cool.
- Drain the blister by piercing the top layer of skin and gently pushing the fluid out.
- Pat the area dry and bandage it.

See **FIGURE 11.22** for the steps for treating blisters.

TREATING BLISTERS

1.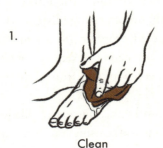

Clean

2.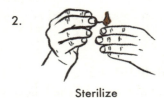

Sterilize

3.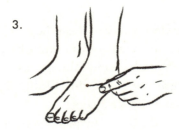

Pierce

4.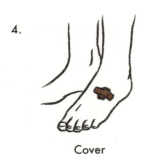

Cover

Figure 11.22

NATURAL MATERIALS FOR PREVENTING AND TREATING BLISTERS

Many fluffy leaves like the mullein can be used as padding to help comfort an area with a hot spot before it becomes a full blister.

Locust thorns will work to drain a blister that has already developed, and you can use pine sap to close the wound. The same mullein leaves will work as a bandage if you have gotten to the point of tearing a blister open. See **FIGURE 11.23** for an example of mullein.

MULLEIN

Figure 11.23

Commonly we are burned from things like hot implements off the fire or from embers. Most of these will not be serious burns.

If you experience a burn, first stop the burning: drop the skillet or put out the sparks that landed on you. Then, you need to cool the burn itself. If water is available, use that. Use the cleanest water available. If you're not near a water source, use cool soil, wet leaves or moss, or other natural means to cool the wound. Before you place these on the wound, cover it with plastic.

The main thing is to keep the burned skin moist and covered. The gel at the base of a cattail shoot is a decent local anesthetic and will relieve some pain as well as keep it moist if the burn is also covered with a bandage. See **FIGURE 11.24** for an example of a cattail.

For a moist dressing, dampen clean cloth dressings such as a bandana, T-shirt, or gauze if you have them. For more serious burns, such as very deep burns or burns that cover a large amount of skin, medical help should be sought immediately.

Bushcraft Tip

If the burn is severe (10 percent of the body or more), don't try to cool the burn using water as this could lead to hypothermia. Instead, focus on dressing the burn and getting immediate help.

CATTAIL

Figure 11.24

If you're out in the wild, it's inevitable that you'll get bitten or stung eventually. You can reduce the likelihood by wearing long-sleeved shirts and long pants.

TREATING SPIDER BITES

While most spider bites aren't dangerous to humans, a few spiders do have fangs long enough to pierce human skin and venom toxic enough to make humans sick. These include the black widow, tarantula, and brown recluse spiders. It's extremely rare to die from a spider bite in North America, but the venom can make you sick enough to warrant professional medical attention. See **FIGURE 11.25** for an example of what a spider bite looks like.

If you're bitten by a spider, clean the bite using soap and clean water. Use cold packs to reduce swelling and ease the pain. Look for tulip poplars and make a poultice from the leaves. A poultice is simply heated or cooled plant material that is applied directly to the affected area and covered with a bandage. The material can also be used raw in the form of a spit poultice where the material is chewed up and then applied from the mouth directly to the wound site and bandaged. You can also do this with plantain or black walnut leaves. See **FIGURE 11.26** for an example of a tulip poplar, **FIGURE 11.27** for an example of a plantain, and **FIGURE 11.28** for an example of black walnut.

SPIDER BITE

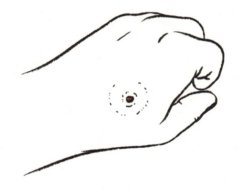

Figure 11.25

TULIP POPLAR

Figure 11.26

PLANTAIN

Figure 11.27

BLACK WALNUT

Figure 11.28

TREATING TICK BITES AND TICK-BORNE ILLNESS

Some ticks carry dangerous diseases, so it's important to do frequent visual inspections of your body when you're out in the wilderness.

Be sure to pay special attention to areas prone to tick bites, such as the ankles and neck. Try not to let any ticks land on you. They are heaviest in clearings near woodlands—such as trails, paths, and open areas that are frequented by larger animals, so pay special attention when traveling in these areas.

See **FIGURE 11.29** for an example of a deer tick.

DEER TICK

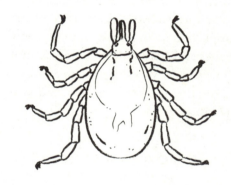

Figure 11.29

If you do get bitten by a tick, remove it immediately. Use tweezers to grasp the tick as close to the skin surface as possible. If you don't have tweezers available, use your fingernails. Then clean the bite with soap and water. Use cold packs to reduce swelling and ease pain. Make sure you've removed the entire tick. Sometimes the body pulls away, but the head remains, which can still cause an infection.

OTHER INSECTS THAT STING

Some people can have severe allergic reactions to stings from bees, wasps, and fire ants, so take care to build camps in areas free of these insects. Become familiar with their habitats. For example, fire ants tend to build their characteristic colony mounds in open areas. Bees prefer living near wildflowers and will build their hives in trees nearby. Wasps make hives in trees, shrubs, and on the outside of buildings.

To treat a sting, remove the stinger (if there is one) then wash the area with soap and water. See **FIGURE 11.30** for an example of how to remove a stinger with tweezers and **FIGURE 11.31** for an example of how to remove a stinger with a credit card or other thin, stiff piece of cardboard or plastic.

REMOVING A STINGER WITH TWEEZERS

Figure 11.30

REMOVING A STINGER WITH A CREDIT CARD

Figure 11.31

To reduce swelling and pain, apply ice or a cold canteen to the bite. Cold water will reduce swelling and can be combined with plant material for a dressing. If you don't have tweezers, you can use a pair of larger locust thorns as probes to remove a stinger. Cattail gel works for local pain. Plantain is a great drawing agent as is crushed charcoal when combined in a bandage.

SNAKES AND SNAKEBITES

In the US, commonly encountered venomous snakes include copperheads, rattlesnakes, and water moccasins. These are so-called pit vipers and have a triangular, flat head; vertical pupils; and a heat-sensitive "pit" located between the eye and nostril. They're usually 3'–4' long but can range from 1'–12'.

If you're bitten, you'll feel pain or burning at the site. If you look carefully, you'll see two puncture wounds from the snake's fangs. The bitten area will swell and start to discolor and the skin may blister. See **FIGURE 11.32** for an example of what a snakebite looks like.

WHAT A SNAKEBITE MAY LOOK LIKE

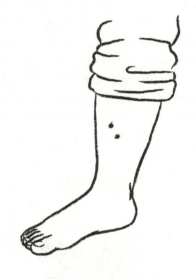

Figure 11.32

If you'll be traveling where venomous snakes are common, it's a good idea to have a Sawyer Extractor with you. A Sawyer Extractor is a suction system used to remove the venom from a bite from underneath your skin. See **FIGURE 11.33** for an example of how to use a Sawyer Extractor.

A SAWYER EXTRACTOR IN USE

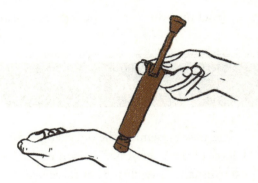

Figure 11.33

Don't try to suction the poison out with your mouth. Don't use a tourniquet (which is unlikely to stop the spread of the poison and could cause further damage). Don't treat the bite with ice packs (which can hurt the skin around the bite). Don't drink alcohol or take aspirin if you've been bitten (both thin the blood). Seek medical help as soon as possible.

ANIMAL BITES

Most of the time in the wild, you won't get near enough to animals for them to bite you. If you do get bitten, clean and bandage the wound and keep an eye on it—look for signs of infection, like red streaks and puffiness. Rabies is the most dangerous risk when bitten in the wild, although in North America this risk is actually low. (Only a handful of cases are reported each year.) That said, if you're bitten by a wild animal you will want to seek professional treatment as soon as possible.

— HARMFUL PLANTS —

Here's a brief introduction to identifying poisonous plants and treating their poisons.

POISON IVY

You may remember the old saying, "Leaves of three, let it be." Poison ivy plants usually have clusters of three broad leaves shaped like spoons. Once you know what it looks like, it's easy to spot. Poison ivy can be a vine or a shrub. The vine can grow low to the ground or it can climb on fences or trees, so you have to keep an eye out for it constantly. See **FIGURE 11.34** for an example of what poison ivy looks like.

POISON IVY

Figure 11.34

POISON OAK

Poison oak looks like oak leaves (thus its name). The leaves are slender with scalloped edges. They grow in odd-numbered groups of three, five, or sometimes seven. In the spring it produces yellow-green flowers that become berries of a similar color in the summer. Like poison ivy, it can grow as a vine or a shrub. See **FIGURE 11.35** for an example of what poison oak looks like.

POISON OAK

Figure 11.35

Poison sumac can be a tree or a shrub, and can grow 20' tall or more. Typically the foliage is not very dense. As a small plant, the leaves grow upward but the branches sag down as the plant reaches full height. Leaves grow in parallel pairs up the stem with a single leaf at the end of each stem. The leaves have an oval shape that comes to a point at the ends. The leaves change color as the seasons change. See **FIGURE 11.36** for an example of what poison sumac looks like.

POISON SUMAC

Figure 11.36

TREATING REACTIONS TO POISON IVY, POISON OAK, AND POISON SUMAC

If you touch any of these plants, their resins will begin to bond to your skin. The process takes about half an hour, so wash your skin with soap and water immediately. Also remove and wash any clothing that has come in contact with the resin. If you are not able to immediately remove the resin, use an alcohol-based cleaner or a commercial preparation to remove the resin. Jewelweed and plantain also aid in the prevention of spread, redness, itching, and swelling. See **FIGURE 11.37** for an example of jewelweed.

JEWELWEED

Figure 11.37

RESCUING AN INJURED PERSON

Sometimes a person in your group may be hurt in such a way as to require rescue, not just treatment. Remember, don't jeopardize your own safety to help someone else.

If you suspect someone in the water is potentially drowning, don't jump in yourself. Instead, try to give him or her something to hold onto, like a tree branch that you extend. If this won't work row or swim out to the person using some sort of flotation device (a raft, a canoe).

Bushcraft Tip

People who are near to drowning don't splash around in the water calling for help (although a tired or distressed swimmer may do this). Someone in the state of active drowning can't even reach for a nearby flotation device. Signs of active drowning include the head being low in the water and tilted back, eyes closed or glassy (not focusing), and not using the legs. The most counterintuitive aspect of drowning is that the swimmer may not seem in distress. If you suspect someone is in trouble, ask, "Are you all right?" If the swimmer can answer, she is probably okay. If not, then she needs help.

Next, determine the extent of injuries before moving the person. Even a short fall—for example, from 3'—can do serious harm. When someone falls more than three times his or her own height, a spine injury is likely. If you need to move someone over distance and the individual can't make it under his or her own power, you can improvise a stretcher. See **FIGURES 11.38 THROUGH 11.41** for examples of improvised stretchers.

BLANKET STRETCHER

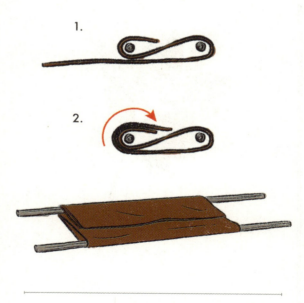

Figure 11.38

BUSHCRAFT ILLUSTRATED

CLOTHING STRETCHER

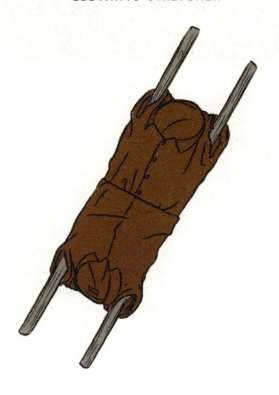

Figure 11.39

Bushcraft Tip

According to the National Institutes of Health, falls and drowning are the most common causes of death for people exploring the wilderness. Use special care when hiking and climbing and when near water.

DUCT TAPE STRETCHER

Figure 11.40

ROPE STRETCHER

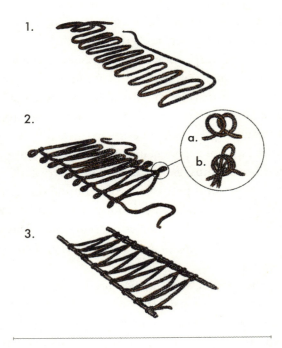

Figure 11.41

— NATURAL MEDICINES —

For some natural medicines or treatments, I use a method called the woodsman's apothecary based on very common trees that are in the Eastern Woodlands. This could be adapted to your area with research.

Becoming a good herbalist can take years of dedication, research, and practical application to master. We just need to know what we can do to make the pain go away or to relieve the swelling from a spider bite or stop some bleeding from an errant knife slice. Some of these solutions we may carry in, but other needs can be harvested from the landscape.

If you understand the natural resources around you, you can use many of them in temporary replacement of treatments that you may keep in your bathroom cabinet at home to treat things like a sore throat, headache, sore muscles, diarrhea, stomach upset, and gas.

For our purposes, we concentrate on a single symptom or action we want to accomplish. If you have a stomachache you probably can figure out why. You're either hungry, ate or drank something that didn't agree with you, or have picked up a virus. Are you experiencing other symptoms like diarrhea, cramps, gas/bloating, vomiting? All of these symptoms probably revolve around one central illness. So really all you must figure out is how to help relieve or counteract the symptoms. This is where knowing the plants in your local area comes into play.

The good news is that you need knowledge of relatively very few plants to take care of lots of things. Plants have two main components: primary metabolites and secondary metabolites. The primaries are what give the plant its growth—the carbohydrates and fibers that help make it a living organism. The secondary metabolites are what we want to understand in our quest for relief. These are the compounds that give the plant taste, make it poison, give it color, and so on. They can also be minerals absorbed from the soil. These are the active components, if you will.

These secondary metabolites can have many different effects on the body both internally and externally, but by using the entire plant and not just a single metabolite or chemical constituent (like many modern pharmaceuticals) you can treat many different things. Simples are herbal preps having only one main ingredient of plant matter.

Let's take a look at something very quickly to help us understand a bit more about herbal energetics (what plants do to our bodies). In herbal applications for this context, we are really trying to treat one symptom with plant matter that has the opposite effect on tissue. In the most simplistic of terms used by the early Greeks, this was called the four humors (wet, dry, cold, hot). If you have a hot condition, you want a cooling effect from the herb and so on. Opposites create balance. This can be quite complicated the more you study and the deeper you get into herbalism, but for starters this is a good basic concept to understand.

The next thing you need to understand is taste. I will use very simple and generic terms here for this discussion. Common tastes are: astringent (drying/puckering), sour (cool), acrid (foul tasting), aromatic (spicy/warm), mucilaginous (wet, creates saliva), and bitter (leaves aftertaste). If you have properly identified the plant, you know if it is safe to place into your mouth. If you are safe tasting the plant, the taste can give you clues as to what this plant will do to you both internally and externally.

Astringent is a good example to look at. If I place a green plant leaf into my mouth, say from a goldenrod, and it dries my mouth out, then I can deduce it is astringent. It may be slightly something else as well, like bitter or acrid, but the drying is the key for this example. If it is drying then wet conditions like bleeding, runny nose, diarrhea (could also be cold or hot) can be treated with it. Some of these would require external use and some internal, so we need to understand how we use the plants.

White oak is an example of an astringent plant. It can be used to stop minor bleeding. See **FIGURE 11.42** for an example of white oak.

WHITE OAK

Figure 11.42

Wild garlic is an aromatic plant. It can be used to relieve shortness of breath. See **FIGURE 11.43** for an example of wild garlic.

WILD GARLIC

Figure 11.43

Dandelion is bitter and can be used as a diuretic. See **FIGURE 11.44** for an example of dandelion.

DANDELION

Figure 11.44

Curly dock is sour, and it can be used for cooling and to relieve inflammation. See **FIGURE 11.45** for an example of curly dock.

CURLY DOCK

Figure 11.45

Boneset is acrid, so it is warming, and can be used as a stimulant. See **FIGURE 11.46** for an example of boneset.

BONESET

Figure 11.46

Sassafras is mucilaginous and is used for moistening. See **FIGURE 11.47** for an example of sassafras.

SASSAFRAS

Figure 11.47

PREPARING HERBS

You want the most simplistic ways to use the plants as you are in the woods. You are only carrying what you need without a lot of frills, so you should be able to prepare and use herbal remedies easily. Remember, just like tinder, medicinals must be processed accordingly to increase surface area. Here are common preparation methods.

- **Just eat it!** If you don't have time for prep and need the plant internally, just consume it. You should have already determined it is safe. Eating too much in most cases will not harm you. If you can't stand to eat too much due to taste, you probably don't need that much anyway. Your body knows. It is not like pills where two is good and five will kill you.
- **Spit poultices.** The plant is macerated in the mouth, mixed with saliva, and held atop the wound with a dressing.
- **Infusion.** Prepare an infusion like a tea. Pour hot water over the herb and cover it to steep for ten to fifteen minutes.
- **Decoction.** A decoction is made up of roots or barks that are boiled in water and strained. Boiling for ten to twenty minutes will suffice if the stock is processed down. Both infusions and decoctions can be gargled or consumed.
- **Fomentation.** Fomentation is done by soaking a rag in hot liquid from an infusion or decoction and applying to the skin.
- **Wash.** Similar to a fomentation a wash is used to rinse an area or flush a wound site.

Now you have some basic information to work with. You can look to what plants to use. Do you need to know every plant in the woods to become effective at treating common ailments? No! You need to have a small list of very common plants that will cover the features we are looking for. Remember you are in the woods for a short time. You don't need to pass a kidney stone (hopefully) or cure a disease (hopefully)!

You are looking for simple treatments for those annoyances that make woods life less enjoyable while recreating. Make a list of things you think could happen that won't necessarily force you to leave but may make for a few uncomfortable days. Examples might include upset stomach, headache, sore throat, constipation, toothache, cuts and abrasions, and burns. Put this list in one column, and try to associate a humor to each condition (dry, wet, cold, hot). In another column use the list of tastes for plants, and place them opposite the condition they would treat. Remember the principle of opposites we spoke about earlier.

PLANT ENERGETICS

Here are a couple things we should also discuss without getting too involved with plant energetics. One is that aromatic plants and trees will be carminative in nature. That is, they will be digestive system balancers. Remember when you had a sore tummy as a kid and Grandma gave you ginger ale? Ginger is a spicy, warm root that settles the digestive system.

The other thing we should look at is acridity: "nasty makes the best medicine." These plants are likely diaphoretic (make you sweat through warming the body's core). These are the best fever breakers. Yarrow and boneset are classic examples of this, although they both have lots of other redeeming qualities like being powerful astringents (to treat bleeding).

Bitter plants stimulate digestion by increasing bile output but will also be diuretic (expel liquids, make you urinate a lot).

Once you have this list, I would suggest going to the field and finding about ten plants and five trees that you have everywhere and can identify without a problem—in all seasons when it comes to trees. Once you have done this, write this list in a separate column on the same sheet. *Do not* go to the Internet or some herb manual yet! Go back out to the field with your list and taste all the plants you have identified as nonpoisonous. Draw lines to match these with your chart and you will have a good start to understanding things like: gravel root is very astringent and bitter, so it will be a good infusion for diarrhea, runny nose, and stomach upset.

Once you have gone through this process, go back and study what has been written about each plant. Internet research is fine, but make sure anything you research on the web is backed up by a credentialed author. This research will show you the more intimate properties the plant may have that take some time to actually learn and may not be absolutely transparent from taste or appearance alone.

I believe that while there are hundreds of plants out there that will treat simple symptoms in the woods, there are only a few trees. However, a few is all you really need. You can treat almost any ailment in the short term with common trees of your area, and these will be a four-season resource that will be easier to locate when needed.

Bushcraft Tip

If you're suffering from an itch because you got too close to a pile of poison ivy, any plant or tree with a high concentration of tannins will constrict the pores of your skin and help push the oils to the surface where they can be neutralized more easily or scrubbed off. Oaks, both red and white, have high concentrations of tannins even in the leaves. You can create a cold infusion or a tea that will help as a wash. However, do not use warm liquid on an itch as this will only serve to aggravate the condition.

NEXT-STEP TOOLS

THE KNIFE, AXE, and saw are the three main tools used by anyone practicing bushcraft. However, as you learned in Chapter 2, you may need to carry in additional or more specialized tools to practice some specific applications in field craft or certain types of finer working. Here you'll learn about the next-step tools you should consider having in your pack.

THE FIVE-TOOL RULE

To process wood, and bark in particular, you must do five things and you must carry tools that allow you to accomplish them. Your tools will be dictated by the size of your kit, the projects planned, and space and weight allowances. I call this the "Five-Tool Rule." Following is a list of the tools most often used to accomplish these five tasks.

1. Severing the grain: saw, axe, knife, mocotaugan, draw knife, spoon knife, gouge
2. Splitting the wood with the grain: axe, knife
3. Shaping the wood: axe, knife, mocotaugan
4. Boring the wood: knife, awl, auger
5. Making concavities: knife, mocotaugan, gouge, spoon knife

As you can see, the three main tools we discussed (knife, saw, and axe) plus a backup carving or whittling knife will perform three of those functions well, and the other two to some extent, but for creating objects more easily and for better results you should sometimes have a couple of other options to make a neater job of things.

CARVING TOOLS

A carving knife is a great tool to add to your pack. Choose one that has a blade that enables finer work for shaping as well. A nice thin profile and shorter blade length make the optimal tool. The Morakniv company of Sweden has been making knives for more than 120 years and I generally use a Mora 120 for this purpose. See **FIGURE APPENDIX.1** for an example of a carving knife.

Bushcraft Tip

Safe handling practices with your knife in the field are of utmost importance. Practice with your knife will make you more comfortable, but don't replace caution with complacency. A sharp knife is a double-edged sword: capable of the finest of carving tasks, but also capable of inflicting a deep wound and leaving permanent damage.

CARVING KNIFE

Figure Appendix.1

TOOLS FOR MAKING CONCAVITIES

These next tools are truly indispensable if you plan to do much craft work during your outings. You will want some type of tool specialized at creating concavities in wood. Bent and curved tools accomplish tasks in woodcraft that a straight tool cannot. They can be bent to reach a certain angle, or curved to create a concave or curved cut into the wood. For this you could choose something like a gouge or a more versatile tool like a bent knife.

The bent knife can go by many names and has many styles depending on where it developed and what it was used for. This tool can easily be carried in an everyday pack and will give you more precision (and enjoyment) when crafting things like spoons, bowls, cups (kuksas), and more. Here you'll learn about two basic bent tools: the spoon or hook knife and a tool called the mocotaugan.

SPOON KNIFE

The spoon knife or hook knife is a tool used throughout Europe and Scandinavia to fashion concavities when working wood. It is generally used to cut across the grain when making things like spoons. It is a simple knife with a bent blade that is generally beveled on the bottom side to help lift itself back out of the wood. There are many shapes and sizes of these tools and some are even made to use with two hands by holding the workpiece in a vise of sorts. As with most tools, many of these knives were built or modified for the user and they are made both left- and right-handed. The Morakniv company of Sweden has specific knives such as the 164, which is a great general purpose spoon knife. See **FIGURES APPENDIX.2 AND APPENDIX.3** for examples of various spoon knives.

SPOON KNIFE, VERSION 1

Figure Appendix.2

SPOON KNIFE, VERSION 2

Figure Appendix.3

Uniquely created in North America, the mocotaugan is a favored tool of indigenous peoples especially in the northern regions of the US and Canada. The First Nation peoples consider this tool one of the most important. "Crooked knife" was another name for this bent tool. I cannot in this short space do justice to this tool, its many uses, or its absolute sacred importance to the peoples who used it, but I will try to make a brief explanation. You can seek further information from the book *Mocotaugan* by Russell Jalbert and Ned Jalbert.

Unlike the spoon knife, the mocotaugan is sharpened on the upper edge, has a fairly long blade of 3"–4", and has an acute angle on its commonly decorative handle. It is truly a multifunctional tool designed specifically for the intent of its user. To understand all the different configurations of these tools we must look at what the tool was commonly used for. The mocotaugan was used for fabricating many everyday items with natural materials, from canoe parts and paddles to snow shoes, drinking vessels, and utensils. This tool, unlike any other, is meant to be used one handed, held with the palm up, and cutting toward the body while the workpiece is held in the other hand. If you look at a project like a canoe paddle that is tapered from the center to the outside of the blade, you can see where a tool of this length would be ideal for working with the grain to remove large shavings on opposite faces of the paddle.

See **FIGURES APPENDIX.4 AND APPENDIX.5** for examples of various mocotaugans.

MOCOTAUGAN, VERSION 1

Figure Appendix.4

MOCOTAUGAN, VERSION 2

Figure Appendix.5

Modern hybrid tools that are a combination of the spoon knife and the mocotaugan are also finding their way into the bushcrafter's kit and have distinct advantages over either of these knives on their own. These hybrids have a shallower learning curve and a slightly more comfortable feel for the beginner using these tools. Ben & Lois Orford, a British company, makes a modern spoon knife with about 2½" of blade that is upturned yet sharpened on the bottom of the blade that I find very useful.

Bent tools are truly multifunctional and will do most things a carving knife will do if held in a fist grip. They make fine shavings for fire kindling and can be used upside down for feathering sticks. Or use them in the same manner as a traditional spoon knife if you desire, as well as a palm-upward draw knife action for shaping wood. I recommend further research on these tools and their origins as well as use if it is of interest to you.

Bushcraft Tip

Belt pouches, usually made of leather, are where the bushcrafter keeps his or her main fire kit and possibly a spare carving knife or jackknife. It is your wallet, so to speak, used to carry the most important items you may need, especially if you have left everything else behind at camp or if you lose your supplies. The size of this pouch can vary, but you don't want it so big as to become cumbersome while moving about.

A gouge is like a chisel but is generally beveled on the bottom side and curved, which is known as the sweep (depth of the curve). A gouge's sweep is numbered from 0 to 10, with 10 being the deepest curve and 0 being almost flat. A label giving information on its sweep also provides its width in millimeters. For example, a gouge labeled as 7/35 means the gouge has a #7 sweep and is 35 mm in width. I use this number because it is a good general use gouge for craft work.

Some gouges can be longer for use on a lathe or with a mallet and some are smaller with a bulbous handle called a palm gouge. Some of them may also be bent. These are aptly called bent gouges and they are handy for creating longer, deeper openings like you'd need for a large bowl. The main disadvantage is that gouges are a single function item, unlike the aforementioned mocotaugan or the hybrids. The advantage is leverage of a heavier tool and the ability of most to use a mallet to assist in waste stock removal. See **FIGURES APPENDIX.6 THROUGH APPENDIX.8** for examples of various types of gouges.

GOUGE

Figure Appendix.6

PALM GOUGE

Figure Appendix.7

BENT GOUGE

Figure Appendix.8

Adzes have been used for making concavities as well as cutting and shaping wood, depending on whether the tool is straight or curved. An adze employs a blade set perpendicular to the handle at varying degrees of angle and can be straight-bladed or curved. The curved adze is most commonly used for carving out larger concavities on objects from bowls to canoes.

An adze can be improvised from a tree branch by adding a piece of forged and sharpened metal, and centuries ago they were made with stone blades, done if needed on the fly. Like the gouge, adzes are beveled only on one side of the blade. This can be to the outside or the inside. It is best to use an outside bevel on an adze as this will tend to ride better on the curvatures of things like bowls and will not tend to dig deeper into the grain the way a chisel would if used bevel-side up. See **FIGURES APPENDIX.9 AND APPENDIX.10** for examples of types of adzes.

SMALL BOWL ADZE

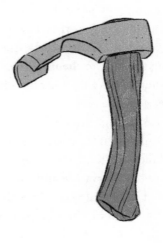

Figure Appendix.9

IMPROVISED ADZE

Figure Appendix.10

Bent and curved tools are cared for in the same manner as any knife, for the most part. Just remember that they have a single bevel, so you should work the beveled edge by pushing the burr to the unbeveled edge first and then remove the burr by rotating strokes between the two.

As with knives, a strop is best for honing work unless you have damaged or severely dulled the tool. The issue with these tools is the curvature and this can be addressed in several ways. Something round like a dowel can be wrapped in abrasive or leather to remove the burr, and a flat board can be used following the bevel. In the case of a longer blade that is beveled on the top, use something flexible like a thick folded leather pad or a dowel that is wrapped. As with knives, a stropping compound followed by bare leather works best. Tormek is the compound I generally use.

Bushcraft Tip

In sharpening a blade, carefully consider its current condition. If you use too coarse an abrasive, you are wasting a resource by removing more metal from the blade than needed, causing unnecessary wear. If you properly care for your blade, it should never take more than fine sharpening, honing, and stropping to maintain a keen cutting edge.

— AWLS —

Awls can easily be improvised from bone if needed by sharpening something like a cannon bone on a coarse stone, and were one of the earliest tools used for making things like clothing. Here we'll take a look at different types of awls and what they're used for in the woods.

TRADE AWL

A small trade awl, or crooked awl, similar to that traded by the Hudson's Bay Company in the early years of the US is a great addition to your kit. The trade awl is a piercing device with two pointed ends and a crook of offset in the middle. With this tool it is very easy to bore small holes in things like bark for lacing, punch holes in leather, or make small holes in wood for pinning or lacing like pack frame components. You can easily add a handle to a trade awl for comfort in use by cutting a green (live) branch with a soft, pithy center and then pressing one end of the trade awl firmly into it. See **FIGURE APPENDIX.11** for an example of a trade awl.

TRADE AWL

Figure Appendix.11

STRAIGHT AWL

Note that any awl accomplishes the same end result: boring holes. The straight awl is not bent like the trade awl, and is generally only sharp at one end. A straight awl can be fashioned from even a nail easily enough by mounting it to a wooden handle. See **FIGURES APPENDIX.12 AND APPENDIX.13** for examples of straight awls.

NAIL AWL

Figure Appendix.12

PUNCH AWL

Figure Appendix.13

STITCH AWLS

Stitch awls, also called sewing awls, generally include a heavy needle with an eye near the tip that is used for both piercing and sewing things like leather and fabrics. Most incorporate some type of heavy thread, generally waxed, within the wood handle and sometimes multiple needles for different tasks as well. This tool will not be what you want when working with barks, etc. However, the stitch awl is useful for making repairs in gear. See **FIGURE APPENDIX.14** for an example of a stitch awl.

STITCH AWL

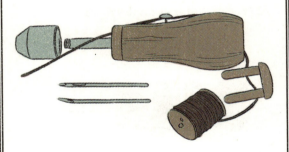

Figure Appendix.14

BONE AWL

The bone awl is a miscellaneous tool used for boring holes in leather, bark, or thin wood as one of the Five-Tool Rule tools. See **FIGURE APPENDIX.15** for an example of a bone awl.

BONE AWL

Figure Appendix.15

━ AUGER ━

Augers are tools that are used similarly to a drill, but are designed specifically for wood boring. They come in sizes ranging commonly from ¼"–2", although the larger the bit diameter, the larger the handle employed to operate it. To use these tools you can connect the brace or auger bits into a common brace, which is the handle of the auger. See **FIGURES APPENDIX.16 AND APPENDIX.17** for an example of a common brace and a selection of brace bits.

BRACE

BRACE BITS

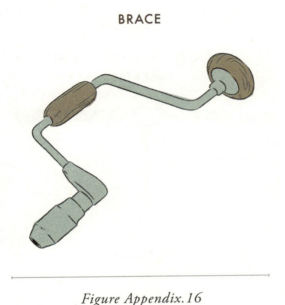

Figure Appendix.16

Figure Appendix.17

Recently people in the bushcraft community have begun to improvise commonly used augers to make this tool easier to carry into the bush than a full set of bits and braces. To make a Scotch eye auger, they weld a ring to the top of an auger bit and then create an auger bit adapter.

A simple auger bit adapter can be made by screwing a ¼" reducer into a T shape of ¾" black iron pipe.

Then take an old auger bit for a form and place it in a vise securely. Heat the reducer to red hot with a torch, then pound it into the shank at the top of the auger bit in order to create a sound fit.

After your adapter has cooled, insert a stick through the upper T and plug in any bit size you desire, up to 1", for boring with no trouble. See **FIGURE APPENDIX.18** for an example of a Scotch eye auger and **FIGURE APPENDIX.19** for an example of an auger bit adapter.

SCOTCH EYE AUGER

Figure Appendix.18

T ADAPTER WITH AUGER BIT INSERTED

Figure Appendix.19

US/Metric Conversion Chart

VOLUME CONVERSIONS

US Volume Measure	Metric Equivalent
⅛ teaspoon	0.5 milliliter
¼ teaspoon	1 milliliter
½ teaspoon	2 milliliters
1 teaspoon	5 milliliters
½ tablespoon	7 milliliters
1 tablespoon (3 teaspoons)	15 milliliters
2 tablespoons (1 fluid ounce)	30 milliliters
¼ cup (4 tablespoons)	60 milliliters
⅓ cup	90 milliliters
½ cup (4 fluid ounces)	125 milliliters
⅔ cup	160 milliliters
¾ cup (6 fluid ounces)	180 milliliters
1 cup (16 tablespoons)	250 milliliters
1 pint (2 cups)	500 milliliters
1 quart (4 cups)	1 liter (about)

LENGTH CONVERSIONS

US Length Measure	Metric Equivalent
¼ inch	0.6 centimeters
½ inch	1.2 centimeters
¾ inch	1.9 centimeters
1 inch	2.5 centimeters
1½ inches	3.8 centimeters
1 foot	0.3 meters
1 yard	0.9 meters

WEIGHT CONVERSIONS

US Weight Measure	Metric Equivalent
½ ounce	15 grams
1 ounce	30 grams
2 ounces	60 grams
3 ounces	85 grams
¼ pound (4 ounces)	115 grams
½ pound (8 ounces)	225 grams
¾ pound (12 ounces)	340 grams
1 pound (16 ounces)	454 grams

Index

About the Author

Dave Canterbury is the co-owner and supervising instructor at The Pathfinder School, which *USA TODAY* named one of the top twelve survival schools in the United States. He has been published in *Self Reliance Illustrated*, *The New Pioneer*, *American Frontiersman*, and *Trapper's World*. Dave is the *New York Times* bestselling author of *Bushcraft 101*; *Advanced Bushcraft*; *The Bushcraft Field Guide to Trapping, Gathering, & Cooking in the Wild*; and *Bushcraft First Aid*.

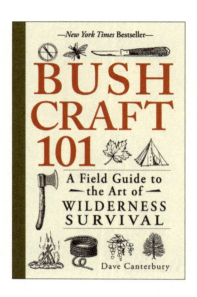

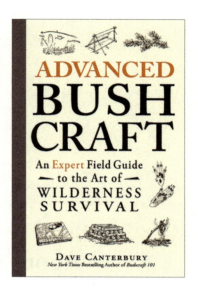

Your Ultimate Resources for — Experiencing the —

BACKCOUNTRY!

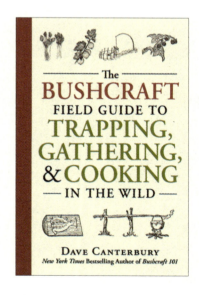

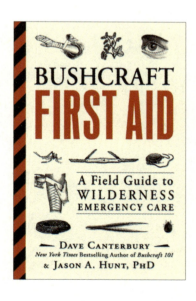

PICK UP OR DOWNLOAD YOUR COPIES TODAY!